Review of the Splendid Perches, *Callanthias*

Frontispiece. *Callanthias allporti.* Fiordland, New Zealand. Photograph by Quentin Bennett, published in Kuiter (2004).

Review of the Splendid Perches, *Callanthias* (Percoidei: Callanthiidae)

William D. Anderson Jr.
Grice Marine Biological Laboratory
College of Charleston
205 Fort Johnson
Charleston, South Carolina 29412-9110
e-mail: andersonwd@cofc.edu

G. David Johnson and Carole C. Baldwin
Department of Vertebrate Zoology
National Museum of Natural History
Smithsonian Institution
Washington, D.C. 20560
e-mail: johnsond@si.edu and baldwinc@si.edu

American Philosophical Society
Philadelphia • 2015

TRANSACTIONS
of the
American Philosophical Society
Held at Philadelphia
For Promoting Useful Knowledge
Volume 105, Part 3

ISBN: 978-1-60618-053-2
US ISSN: 0065-9746

Library of Congress Cataloging-in Publication Data

Anderson, William D. (William Dewey), 1933-
Review of the splendid perches, Callanthias (Percoidei: Callanthiidae) / William D. Anderson, Jr., Grice Marine Biological Laboratory, College of Charleston, 205 Fort Johnson, Charleston, South Carolina ; G. David Johnson and Carole C. Baldwin, Department of Vertebrate Zoology, National Museum of Natural History, Smithsonian, Institution, Washington, D.C.
pages cm. – (Transactions of the American Philosophical Society ; volume 105, part 3)
Includes bibliographical references and index.
ISBN 978-1-60618-053-2 (alk. paper)
1. Perch. I. Johnson, G. David. II. Baldwin, Carole C. III. Title.
QL638.P4A53 2015
597'.73 – dc23
2015028325

Book composition: BookComp, Inc.
Book printing: Sterling Pierce Co. Inc.

Front Cover. *Callanthias australis.* Male in cave; Montague Island, New South Wales, Australia; depth 25 meters. Photograph by Rudie H. Kuiter, published in Kuiter (2004).

Back Cover. *Callanthias australis.* Male with "unusual deep water colouration;" off Bate Bay, New South Wales, Australia; depth ~ 120 meters. Photograph by Ken Graham, published in Kuiter (2004).

Dedicated to the many ichthyological colleagues
who provided assistance and most of all to the fishes who made it possible.

And yet I say unto you, That even Solomon in all his glory was not arrayed like one of these.

Matthew 6:29 (KJV)

CONTENTS

List of Plates xi

List of Figures xiii

List of Tables xv

List of Maps xvii

Preface xix

Acknowledgments xxi

Introduction 1

Methods and Abbreviations 3

Callanthias 5

Key to the Species of *Callanthias* 11

Callanthias allporti 13

Callanthias australis 17

Callanthias japonicus 25

Callanthias legras 29

Callanthias parini 33

Callanthias platei 37

Callanthias ruber 41

Other Reports of *Callanthias* 45

Pseudobranchial Filaments 46

Modified Midlateral Body Scales 48

Geographic Distribution 49

Discussion 49

Literature Cited 51

Plates 65

Figures 73

Tables 97

Maps 117

Index 123

LIST OF PLATES

Plate 1. *Callanthias allporti.*

Plate 2. *Callanthias australis.*

Plate 3. *Callanthias japonicus.*

Plate 4. *Callanthias legras.*

Plate 5. *Callanthias parini.*

Plate 6. *Callanthias platei.*

Plate 7. *Callanthias ruber.*

Plate 8. *Callanthias* sp.

LIST OF FIGURES

Figure 1. Nasal lamellae.

Figure 2. Modified midlateral body scales.

Figure 3. Configurations of supraneural bones, anterior neural spines, and anterior dorsal pterygiophores in callanthiid fishes.

Figure 4. Pseudobranch.

Figure 5. Ctenoid scales with only marginal cteni.

Figure 6. Comparison of length of first spine in anal fin versus standard length in *Callanthias australis* and *C. japonicus.*

Figure 7. Comparison of length of second spine in anal fin versus standard length in *Callanthias australis* and *C. japonicus.*

Figure 8. Comparison of length of penultimate soft ray in dorsal fin versus standard length in *Callanthias australis* and *C. japonicus.*

Figure 9. Comparison of length of penultimate soft ray in anal fin versus standard length in *Callanthias australis* and *C. japonicus.*

Figure 10. Comparison of length of upper jaw versus standard length in *Callanthias australis* and *C. platei.*

Figure 11. Comparison of length of first spine in anal fin versus standard length in *Callanthias australis* and *C. platei.*

Figure 12. Comparison of length of penultimate soft ray in dorsal fin versus standard length in *Callanthias australis* and *C. platei.*

Figure 13. Comparison of length of penultimate soft ray in anal fin versus standard length in *Callanthias australis* and *C. platei.*

Figure 14. Comparison of length of upper jaw versus standard length in *Callanthias japonicus* and *C. platei.*

Figure 15. Comparison of predorsal length versus standard length in *Callanthias japonicus* and *C. platei.*

Figure 16. Comparison of length of first spine in anal fin versus standard length in *Callanthias japonicus* and *C. platei.*

Figure 17. Comparison of length of penultimate soft ray in dorsal fin versus standard length in *Callanthias japonicus* and *C. platei.*

Figure 18. Length–weight relationship for *Callanthias parini.*

Figure 19. Relationship of number of pseudobranchial filaments to standard length in *Callanthias australis* and *C. japonicus.*

Figure 20. Relationship of number of pseudobranchial filaments to standard length in *Callanthias australis* and *C. platei.*

Figure 21. Relationship of number of pseudobranchial filaments to standard length in *Callanthias platei* and *C. japonicus.*

Figure 22. Relationship of number of pseudobranchial filaments to standard length in *Callanthias legras* and *C. ruber.*

Figure 23. Relationship of number of pseudobranchial filaments to standard length in *Callanthias parini* and *C. allporti.*

LIST OF TABLES

Table 1. Summary of selected characters in species of *Callanthias.*

Table 2. Frequency distributions for numbers of soft rays in the dorsal fin in species of *Callanthias.*

Table 3. Frequency distributions for numbers of soft rays in the anal fin in species of *Callanthias.*

Table 4. Frequency distributions for numbers of rays in the pectoral fin in species of *Callanthias.*

Table 5. Frequency distributions for sums of numbers of pectoral-fin rays from left and right sides of individual specimens in species of *Callanthias.*

Table 6. Frequency distributions for total numbers of gillrakers on first arch in species of *Callanthias.*

Table 7. Frequency distributions for numbers of tubed lateral-line scales in species of *Callanthias.*

Table 8. Frequency distributions for sums of numbers of tubed lateral-line scales from left and right sides in individual specimens of species of *Callanthias.*

Table 9. Frequency distributions for numbers of lateral-line scales posterior to base of ultimate dorsal soft ray in species of *Callanthias.*

Table 10. Frequency distributions for sums of numbers of gillrakers on first arch plus numbers of tubed lateral-line scales in individual specimens of species of *Callanthias.*

Table 11. Frequency distributions for numbers of mid-body lateral scales in species of *Callanthias.*

Table 12. Frequency distributions for numbers of circum-caudal-peduncular scales in species of *Callanthias.*

Table 13. Frequency distributions for numbers of scales between anal-fin origin and lateral line in species of *Callanthias.*

Table 14. Frequency distributions for numbers of rows of cheek scales in species of *Callanthias.*

Table 15. Frequency distributions for numbers of pseudobranchial filaments in species of *Callanthias.*

Table 16. Frequency distributions for numbers of procurrent caudal-fin rays in species of *Callanthias.*

Table 17. Frequency distributions for numbers of epineural and epural bones and trisegmental pterygiophores in species of *Callanthias.*

Table 18. Comparisons of morphometric data in four species of *Callanthias* that usually have 10 soft rays in both dorsal and anal fins.

Table 19. Comparisons of morphometric data in three species of *Callanthias* that usually have 11 soft rays in both dorsal and anal fins.

Table 20. *Callanthias:* all seven species—dimorphisms (trimorphism in *C. australis*).

LIST OF MAPS

Map 1. Localities of capture for specimens of *Callanthias allporti* and *Callanthias australis* examined in this study.

Map 2. Localities of capture for specimens of *Callanthias japonicus* examined in this study.

Map 3. Localities of capture for specimens of *Callanthias ruber* and *Callanthias legras* examined in this study.

Map 4. Localities of capture for specimens of *Callanthias parini* and *Callanthias platei* examined in this study.

Map 5. Localities of capture for all specimens of *Callanthias* examined in this study.

PREFACE

The family Callanthiidae contains two genera, *Callanthias* (with seven species) and *Grammatonotus* (with six nominal species). We provide characters that distinguish callanthiids from other percoids and that distinguish *Callanthias* from *Grammatonotus,* as well as descriptions of *Callanthias* and its seven species, a key to the species of *Callanthias,* and comments on other aspects of the biology of the species of the genus.

ACKNOWLEDGMENTS

The following assisted us in numerous ways, including providing space to work, donating specimens, sending specimens on loan, supplying information on specimens and nomenclature, and furnishing literature: Gerald R. Allen, Conchita Allué, Kunio Amaoka, Eric Anderson, Peter Bartsch, Marie-Louise Bauchot, the late Adam Ben-Tuvia, Jack van Berkel, the late E. Bertelsen, the late M. Boeseman, Dianne J. Bray, Ralf Britz, David Catania, William N. Eschmeyer, Anne W. Everly, William L. Fink, Pierre Fourmanoir, Daniel Golani, Martin F. Gomon, J. P. Gosse, Alastair Graham, Graham S. Hardy, Karsten E. Hartel, Phillip C. Heemstra, Mandy L. Holloway, P. Alexander Hulley, Jeff Johnson, the late Robert K. Johnson, Susan L. Jewett, Tsutomu Kanayama, the late Masao Katayama, Richard van der Laan, Georges Lenglet, Keiichi Matsuura, Mark A. McGrouther, Anthony G. Miskiewicz, Kenji Mochizuki, Glenn Moore, John Moreland, Bruce C. Mundy, Kazuhiro Nakaya, Jørgen Nielsen, M. J. P. van Oijen, Lisa Palmer, the late Nikolai V. Parin, John R. Paxton, Alfred Post, Tarmo A. Raadik, John E. Randall, Jacques Rivaton, Clive Roberts, Mary Anne Rogers, Mark Sabaj, Kwang-Tsao Shao, Jeffrey A. Seigel, the late Nick Sinclair, Shirleen Smith, William F. Smith-Vaniz, Andrew Stewart, Donald J. Stewart, the late Yoshiaki Tominaga, Thomas Trnski, H. J. Walker Jr., the late Alwyne Wheeler, Horst Wilkens, and Jeffrey T. Williams.

Warren Farrelly, Phillip C. Heemstra, Avi Klapfer, James Maclaine, and the late Nikolai V. Parin provided photographs; Savannah Gilmore scanned photographic transparencies; the late James F. McKinney and Sandra Raredon furnished photographs and radiographs; the late Eugenia B. Böhlke, Patrick Campbell, Robin Curry, Michael Kim, Dorian R. McMillan, John C. McGovern, Michael D. Mullaney Jr., Whitney Stahl, Robin Stobbs, and John B. Wise contributed radiographs; Robert Ashcraft made scanning electron photomicrographs; William A. Roumillat made and examined histological sections of gonads; Rebecca Anderson Durst plotted data; and Gabe Sataloff produced the maps. Quentin Bennett, Malcolm Francis, Ken Grahm, Rudie H. Kuiter, and the South African Institute for Aquatic Biodiversity allowed us to use published illustrations. Figure 4 was modified and reprinted with permission of Elsevier Books, Amsterdam, from W. Waser (2011), Root effect: Root effect definition, functional role in oxygen delivery to the eye and swimbladder, in A. Farrell (editor), Encyclopedia of fish physiology:

From genome to environment, 2:929–934, figs. 4 & 5. Improvements of our translations into English were provided by William D. Anderson III (German), Isaure De Buron-Connors (French), and Norma J. Salcedo (Spanish). Theodore W. Pietsch commented on a short section of the manuscript, and William F. Smith-Vaniz and Jeffrey T. Williams critically read the entire manuscript. Funding in support of this research was provided through the generous assistance of the Herbert R. and Evelyn Axelrod Endowment Fund for systematic ichthyology. Mary McDonald, Editor and Director of Publications, American Philosophical Society, and Nicholle Lutz, Production Editor, BookComp, Inc., guided the manuscript through the publication process. This is contribution number 441 of the Grice Marine Biological Laboratory, College of Charleston.

INTRODUCTION

The splendid perches, *Callanthias*, make up one of two genera in the marine perciform family Callanthiidae. The seven species of these brightly colored, often stunning, planktivorous fishes are found in moderately deep waters, most commonly around rocky reefs and pinnacles. As suggested by their scientific name, they show some resemblance to members of the unrelated serranid subfamily Anthiinae. Our initial interest in the splendid perches emanated not from their spectacular coloration but from specific features of their morphology and their bearing on possible relationships to other perciform fishes. When the second author was a graduate student at the Scripps Institution of Oceanography, he conducted a wide survey of the osteology of the caudal fin and its supporting elements in perciform fishes. One of the results of that survey was the discovery of an undescribed character in the caudal fin of many perciforms (Johnson, 1975); another was the beginning of a research program on the osteology of a broad array of fishes, including the Callanthiidae. In 1978, he moved to Charleston to work for the South Carolina Department of Natural Resources (DNR), and one consequence of that move was recruiting the first author to join forces with him to study the family Callanthiidae. A few years later the third author, who was then a graduate student at the Grice Marine Biological Laboratory (near the DNR laboratory), joined the first two investigators and made major contributions to the study.

Various authors have assigned *Callanthias* Lowe, 1839, to the Serranidae. For example, Tortonese (1972:80) wrote that "At present, *Callanthias* is better . . . provisionally considered as an highly aberrant genus of the family Serranidae." Gilbert (1905:618) described *Grammatonotus*, placed it in the Serranidae, and stated that it is "closely allied to *Callanthias*." We concur with Gilbert on the close relationship of the two genera but agree with Gosline (1966:91, 95) that they do not belong in the Serranidae. Böhlke (1960:7–8) considered *Grammatonotus* to be related to *Lipogramma* (Grammatidae): "Apparently the Hawaiian *Grammatonotus* Gilbert is the closest described relative of *Lipogramma*" (p. 7). Springer (1982:47) considered both *Callanthias* and *Grammatonotus* to be representatives of the Grammatidae but wrote that "there is little evidence to unite" the five genera he included in that family. Later Gill and Mooi (1993:329) concluded that *Gramma* and *Lipogramma* are the only genera in the Grammatidae. Fourmanoir (1981) raised the Callanthiinae, regarded by Ogilby (1899) who proposed the name, Fowler (1907), Katayama (1959, 1960a, 1960b), and Katayama et al. (1982) as a subfamily of the Serranidae, to the familial level, and Johnson (1984) and Anderson and Johnson (1984) agreed with this, including both *Callanthias* and *Grammatonotus* in the Callanthiidae. The species of the two callanthiid genera, *Callanthias* and *Grammatonotus* (*Parabarossia* Kotthaus, 1976, is a junior synonym) share three characters, a combination that is unusual among percoid fishes: nasal organ with poorly developed lamellae (Figure 1), presence of modified scales with unique ornamentation along body midlaterally (Figure 2), and lateral line running along base of dorsal fin to terminate near base of ultimate dorsal soft ray or continuing posteriorly on dorsolateral surface of caudal peduncle (Anderson and Johnson, 1984; Johnson, 1984). Gill and Mooi (1993:329) offered what may be an additional synapomorphy for the two genera: "presence of a well-developed median frontal crest, with an associated elongation of the ossified sensory canal that serves the median posterior interorbital pore." In addition, the species of those genera have an unusual arrangement of the supraneural bones in which the bones do not interdigitate with the neural spines; instead, they are oriented more or less obliquely, with their proximal ends usually terminating anterior to or dorsal to distal end of anteriormost neural spine (Figure 3). Springer and Johnson (2004:158) found no substantive differences between *Callanthias* and *Grammatonotus* in the skeletal structure of the dorsal part of the gill arches.

METHODS AND ABBREVIATIONS

We used Eschmeyer's electronic version of the *Catalog of Fishes* to check our literature citations for dates of publication, authorships, spellings, and related items. Characters in the generic diagnosis form part of the generic description and are not repeated unless necessary for clarification. Similarly, in each species account, characters in the generic and species diagnoses and generic description form part of the species description and are not repeated unless necessary for clarification. Counts and measurements were made following Hubbs and Lagler (1958) except as noted. Lateral-line scales were counted on both sides of each specimen when possible. Other scale counts, with exception of those around the caudal peduncle, were made on either side depending on condition of the specimen. Midbody lateral scales were counted along a horizontal line extending from gill opening to middle of structural base of caudal fin. In making counts of rows of cheek scales, rows of scales above lateral line, and scales above and below lateral line, we excluded small scales at orbit and at bases of dorsal and anal fins. Rows of cheek scales were difficult to count because of missing scales and the irregularity of the rows. The count of scales below lateral line was made along a posterodorsal series from anal-fin origin to (but excluding) lateral-line scale. Gillrakers on first gill arch and pseudobranchial filaments were counted on the right side. The first vertebra with a haemal spine was considered the first caudal vertebra; the urostylar vertebra, the last. Measurements were made with needlepoint dial calipers to nearest 0.1 mm. Those from anterior end of snout were taken from premaxillary symphysis; those involving orbit (snout length, orbit diameter, interorbital width, and postorbital length of head) were of bony orbit. Measurement of orbit was of horizontal diameter. Depth of body was measured from dorsal-fin origin vertically to ventral midline of body. Pectoral- and pelvic-fin lengths were of longer (either left or right) fin. Lengths of caudal-fin lobes were taken from middle of fin base to distal tips of longest rays. Distance from more posterior rib of last pair of ribs to first haemal spine was measured on radiographs produced on film (as a consequence, there was no discrepancy in size between the specimen and the image on the radiograph). This measurement was taken at the greatest point of separation between rib and haemal spine; damaged or grossly distorted specimens were not measured.

The maps show the positions of capture for material we examined for which latitudes and longitudes were available and for collections where reasonably accurate localities could be determined from other information associated with the specimens studied. In many instances, symbols on maps represent more than one collection.

Institutional abbreviations are AIM (Auckland Museum, New Zealand), AMS (Australian Museum, Sydney), ANSP (Academy of Natural Sciences, Philadelphia), ASIZP (Biodiversity Research Center, Academia Sinica, Taipei, Taiwan), BMNH (Natural History Museum, London), BPBM (Bernice P. Bishop Museum, Honolulu), CAS (California Academy of Sciences, San Francisco), CSIRO (Commonwealth Scientific and Industrial Research Organisation, Hobart, Tasmania), FMNH (Field Museum of Natural History, Chicago), FUMT (Department of Fisheries, University Museum, University of Tokyo), GMBL (Grice Marine Biological Laboratory, College of Charleston), HUJ (Hebrew University, Jerusalem), HUMZ (Hokkaido University, Laboratory of Marine Zoology, Hakodate, Japan), IIPB (Instituto de Ciencias del Mar, Barcelona), IOAN (Institute of Oceanology, Moscow), IRSNB (Institut Royal des Sciences Naturelles de Belgique, Brussels), KA (Edward Percival Field Station, Department of Zoology, University of Canterbury, Kaikoura, New Zealand), LACM (Natural History Museum of Los Angeles County), MCZ (Museum of Comparative Zoology, Harvard University), MNHN (Muséum national d'Histoire naturelle, Paris), NMNZ (Museum of New Zealand Te Papa Tongarewa, Wellington), NMV (Museum Victoria, Melbourne), NSMT (National Science Museum, Tokyo), QM (Queensland Museum, Brisbane), RMNH (Naturalis Biodiversity Center, Leiden, Netherlands), SAIAB (formerly RUSI; South African Institute for Aquatic Biodiversity, Grahamstown), SAM (South African Museum, Cape Town), SIO (Scripps Institution of Oceanography), USNM (National Museum of Natural History, Smithsonian Institution, Washington, D.C.), WAM (Western Australian Museum, Perth), ZMB (Museum für Naturkunde Berlin—Leibniz-Institut für Evolutions- und Biodiversitätsforschung an der Humboldt-Universität zu Berlin), ZMH (Zoological Museum Hamburg), ZMMU (Zoological Museum, Moscow State University), ZMUC (Københavns Universitet, Zoologisk Museum, Vertebrater, Fiskesamlingen, Copenhagen, Denmark), ZSM (Zoologische Staatssammlung München), and ZUMT (Department of Zoology, University Museum, University of Tokyo). Standard length is abbreviated as SL, total length as TL.

CALLANTHIAS LOWE, 1839

Splendid Perches, Goldies, Groppos

Plates 1–8, Figures 1–23, Tables 1–20, Maps 1–5

Callanthias Lowe, 1839:76 (type species *Callanthias paradisaeus* Lowe, 1839:76 [= *C. ruber*], by monotypy).

Anogramma Ogilby, 1899:175 (type species *Callanthias allporti* Günther, 1876:390, by monotypy).

Percanthias Tanaka, 1922:591 (type species *Callanthias japonicus* Franz, 1910:40, pl. 6, fig. 49, by original designation p. 594, also monotypic).

Diagnosis. *Callanthias* can be distinguished from the only other callanthiid genus, *Grammatonotus* Gilbert (type species *G. laysanus* Gilbert, 1905), by the following. Two opercular spines in *Callanthias,* one in *Grammatonotus.* Soft rays in dorsal fin 10 or 11 (very rarely 9 or 12) in *Callanthias,* usually 9 (rarely 8 or 10) in *Grammatonotus.* Soft rays in anal fin 10 or 11 (very rarely 9 or 12) in *Callanthias,* 9 in *Grammatonotus.* Branched caudal-fin rays 15 (8 + 7) in *Callanthias,* 13 (7 + 6) in *Grammatonotus.* Tubed lateral-line scales 21 to 47 in *Callanthias,* 14 to 18 in *Grammatonotus.* Most posterior dorsal procurrent caudal-fin ray articulating with most posterior epural and apparently in most cases also receiving support from fifth hypural in *Callanthias;* support for this element almost always from fifth hypural and only occasionally from both most posterior epural and fifth hypural in *Grammatonotus.* Most posterior ventral procurrent caudal-fin ray articulating with haemal spine of penultimate vertebra in *Callanthias;* this fin ray almost always supported by haemal spine of penultimate vertebra and by parhypural in *Grammatonotus.* Distance from most posterior pleural rib to first haemal spine usually appreciably greater in *Callanthias* than in *Grammatonotus* (*Callanthias:* n = 172; in % SL, range = 1.05 to 4.79, mean = 3.20. *Grammatonotus:* n = 28; in % SL, range = 0.68 to 2.14, mean = 1.63. Anderson and Johnson, 1984:949). Also, *Callanthias* and *Grammatonotus* differ in ornamentation present on modified midlateral body scales (Figure 2).

Description. Meristic data are in Tables 1–17; morphometric data, in Tables 18–20. Dorsal fin not incised at junction of spinous and soft portions. Dorsal-fin rays XI, 9 to 12 (very rarely X spines, usually 10 or 11 soft rays). Anal-fin rays III, 9 to 12 (usually 10 or 11). Pectoral-fin rays 17 to 23 (usually 19–22). Pelvic-fin rays I, 5. Caudal fin almost truncate (except dorsalmost and ventralmost principal rays variously produced), emarginate, lunate, or forked. Principal caudal-fin rays 17 (9 + 8). Procurrent caudal-fin rays 6 to 9 dorsally, 5 to 9 ventrally. Branchiostegal rays 6. Pseudobranch (Figure 4) with 11 to 43 filaments (number of filaments tending to increase with increase in SL). Total number of gillrakers, including rudiments, on first gill arch 29 to 38 (usually 30–36). Lateral series of gillrakers on first gill arch long and slender; medial rakers on first arch and rakers on other arches short.

Lateral line ascending abruptly from its origin near opercle to within a few scale rows of dorsal-fin base. Lateral line terminating near base of ultimate dorsal soft ray or extending as far posteriorly as base of caudal fin (most frequently 1 to 10 lateral-line scales present posterior to base of ultimate dorsal soft ray; see Table 9). Tubed lateral-line scales 21 to 47 (usually 22–41); sum of tubed lateral-line scales from left and right sides of individual specimens 43 to 83 (usually 46–80). Sum of lateral-line scales plus total number of gillrakers on first arch, in individual specimens, 54 to 81 (usually 55–76). Rows of cheek scales 5 to 10. Midbody lateral scales 34 to 49 (usually 36–46). Rows of scales between lateral line and midbase of spinous dorsal fin 1 to 3. Scales between dorsal-fin origin and lateral line 1 to 6 (usually 2–4). Scales between anal-fin origin and lateral line 11 to 20 (usually 12–18). Circum-caudal-peduncular scales 15 to 25.

Vertebrae 24 (10 precaudal + 14 caudal; one specimen of *C. legras* with 15 caudal vertebrae). Parapophyses present on first caudal vertebra. No spur on posteriormost ventral procurrent caudal-fin ray; penultimate ventral procurrent caudal-fin ray not shortened basally (see Johnson, 1975). Parhypural autogenous, with well-developed hypurapophysis; hypural 1 + hypural 2 present as a single unit, with no evidence of ontogenetic fusion; hypural 3 + hypural 4 present as a single unit, with no evidence of ontogenetic fusion; hypural 5 autogenous; epurals 2 or 3; a single uroneural pair (anterior) present. Epineurals associated with first 10 to 16 vertebrae (usually with vertebrae 11 to 15). Ribs on vertebrae 3 through 10. Almost always a single trisegmental pterygiophore associated with dorsal fin and one with anal fin. Configuration of supraneural bones, anterior neural spines, and anterior dorsal pterygiophores difficult to depict in the conventional symbolization of Ahlstrom et al. (1976) because supraneural bones do not actually interdigitate with neural spines; the two supraneural bones oriented more or less obliquely with their proximal ends usually terminating anterior to or dorsal to distal end of anteriormost neural spine (Figure 3).

Body compressed, rather slender to moderately deep. Mouth terminal and oblique; jaws almost equal. Maxilla reaching posteriorly to near middle of eye. Premaxilla protrusile. No supramaxilla. Posterodorsal border of maxilla not covered by infraorbital bones with mouth closed. Interorbital convex to flattened. Anterior naris somewhat remote from eye; posterior naris near eye. Section A_1 of adductor mandibulae simple, without anterodorsal extension. Distal margins of preopercle, interopercle, and subopercle without spines or serrations in juveniles and adults, but larvae have small spines or serrations on those bones (Johnson, 1984:486, table 121; Miskiewicz et al., 2000:280–284). Opercular spines two; ventral spine better developed.

Premaxilla with outer series of conical teeth and usually one to a few small exserted canines or canine-like teeth at anterior end of jaw; inner band of villiform to conical teeth, band expanded near symphysis; no teeth at symphysis. Dentary with series of conical teeth; patch of villiform to conical teeth next to symphysis; one to a few exserted canines at anterior end of jaw; no teeth at symphysis.

Vomerine teeth varying from absent to small to well developed (frequently arranged in a chevron-shaped, crescent-shaped, or triangular patch or transverse band, without posterior prolongation). Palatine with or without teeth; when present teeth small, conical, and best developed anteriorly (infrequently with more robust caniniform teeth anteriorly). No teeth on tongue or pterygoids.

Scales peripheral ctenoid (Roberts, 1993:92, 108); posterior field of a scale with primary and secondary cteni (i.e., no ctenial bases present in posterior field) (Figure 5). Body with midlateral series of modified scales. Secondary squamation varying from absent to poorly developed to well developed (Figure 5). Most of head, including maxilla, dentary, dorsum of snout, and interorbital region heavily covered with scales; anterior part of gular region with or without scales, remainder of gular region and branchiostegal rays and membranes without scales. Membranes of dorsal and anal fins usually without scales, sometimes with scales on anterior fin rays, fin membranes, or both; pectoral- and pelvic-fin bases usually with scales; scales sometimes covering soft rays of the pelvic fin; pelvic axillary scales present; modified scales (interpelvic process) overlapping pelvic-fin bases along midventral line; scales extending onto caudal fin (frequently well out onto fin to cover most of it).

Additional morphology. Katayama (1959) recognized 15 subfamilies (including the Callanthiinae) in the family Serranidae and compared the morphology of representatives of those subfamilies. *Callanthias japonicus* was used as the callanthiine example. Aspects of the anatomy of that species examined and illustrated were maxilla (fig. 1), infraorbital bones (fig. 5), suspensorium and opercular apparatus (fig. 9), hyoid apparatus (fig. 14), cranium (fig. 23), vertebral column (fig. 27), pectoral girdle (fig. 31), pelvic girdle (fig. 32), gas bladder (fig. 35), and alimentary canal and pyloric caeca (fig. 38). Springer and Johnson (2004:158–159, pl. 132) described and illustrated the dorsal gill-arch musculature of *Callanthias allporti* and noted that they found "no substantive differences in the musculature between" *C. allporti* and *C. australis*.

Coloration. Brightly colored fishes with shades of red, orange, yellow, and purple predominant.

Dimorphism. All seven species of *Callanthias* show dimorphism with growth. This is usually most evident in lengths of the caudal-fin lobes (Table 20), but in *C. legras* dimorphism is most distinctive in length of the anal fin and to a degree in lengths of the penultimate soft rays in the dorsal and anal fins and in length of the lower lobe of the caudal fin (Table 20). In addition to the caudal-fin lobes, *C. parini* displays dimorphism in lengths of the dorsal and anal fins and in most of the spines and soft rays in those fins (Table 20). Although our data are limited, lengths of fins and fin rays seem to be correlated with sex—males having longer fins and fin rays than do females. Doak (1972:31) observed courting or spawning males of *C. australis* (identified as *C. allporti*) displaying their dorsal and anal fins, thereby making their bodies appear a third greater in depth. Consequently, there might be a selective advantage for elongation of these fins in adult males.

As can be seen in Table 20, the specimens of *C. australis* examined can be placed in three groups based on lengths of caudal-fin lobes: short, medium, long. Assuming that *C. australis* is protogynous, as appears likely, the group with medium-length caudal-fin lobes may consist of transitional individuals that were undergoing sex change when captured.

Sexuality. Adults of some of the species appear to change sex from female to male (protogyny), a transformation that seems to be accompanied by modifications in fin shapes and in some species changes in coloration (Anderson and Johnson, 1984:948; Kuiter, 2004:7–11; Roberts and Gomon, 2008:549). All species of *Callanthias* may be protogynous.

Early life history. Miskiewicz et al. (2000:280–284) provided an account of callanthiid larvae that includes characters distinguishing *Callanthias* from *Grammatonotus* and an illustration (fig. 64, after Trnski and Miskiewicz, 1998: fig. 54) of four specimens (2.8–6.7 mm) of *Callanthias australis.*

Distribution. *Callanthias* is widely distributed in temperate and subtropical latitudes off continental and insular coasts, being antiequatorial and, except for *C. parini,* almost antitropical. The genus is notably absent from the western Atlantic and most of the Pacific and Indian oceans (see Map 5).

Etymology. *Callanthias* is from Greek: "call" from *kallos* (beauty), "anthias" (a sea fish) from *anthos* (flower). According to Jordan and Evermann (1896:1227), *Anthias* is an "ancient name of some large fish, perhaps the Albacore." Certainly "beautiful flower" is an appropriate sobriquet for these lovely fishes.

KEY TO THE SPECIES OF *CALLANTHIAS*

1a. Soft rays in both dorsal and anal fins almost always 10, very rarely 9 or 11 2

1b. Soft rays in both dorsal and anal fins almost always 11, very rarely 10 or 12 5

2a. Tubed lateral-line scales 36–47, usually 37–42. Secondary squamation usually well developed. Vomerine teeth well developed. . . . . *Callanthias allporti*
(western Pacific Ocean off Australia and New Zealand)

2b. Tubed lateral-line scales 21–36. Secondary squamation absent to poorly developed. Vomerine teeth absent, small, or well developed 3

3a. Circum-caudal-peduncular scales 15–17. Vomerine teeth well developed. Epurals 2, very rarely 3 . . . . *Callanthias legras*
(eastern South Atlantic and western Indian oceans off southern Africa)

3b. Circum-caudal-peduncular scales 18–24, rarely 18. Vomerine teeth moderate to small to absent. Epurals 3, rarely 2 4

4a. Tubed lateral-line scales 24–31, usually 26–29. Circum-caudal-peduncular scales 21–24 (usually 23 or 24) . . . . *Callanthias parini*
(eastern South Pacific on Nazca and Sala y Gómez ridges)

4b. Tubed lateral-line scales 21–26, usually 22–24. Circum-caudal-peduncular scales 18–21 (usually 20). . . . . *Callanthias ruber*
(eastern North Atlantic Ocean, including Mediterranean, Adriatic, and Aegean seas)

5a. Total number of gillrakers on first arch 30–38, mean 33.9. Total number of gillrakers plus number of tubed lateral-line scales in individual specimens 66–77, mean 71.2. Sum of numbers of tubed lateral-line scales from left and right sides of individual specimens 69–83, mean 74.7 . . . . *Callanthias australis*
(western South Pacific and southeastern Indian oceans: Australian–New Zealand region)

5b. Total number of gillrakers on first arch 29–33, mean 31.4. Total number of gillrakers plus number of tubed lateral-line scales in individual specimens 65–73, mean 68.5. Sum of numbers of tubed lateral-line scales from left and right sides of individual specimens 68–80, mean 74.2 . . . . *Callanthias japonicus*
(western North Pacific Ocean: central Japan to southern Taiwan)

5c. Total number of gillrakers on first arch 31–35, mean 32.7. Total number of gillrakers plus number of tubed lateral-line scales in individual specimens 69–76, mean 71.8. Sum of numbers of tubed lateral-line scales from left and right sides of individual specimens 73–83, mean 78.3.. . . . . *Callanthias platei* (eastern South Pacific Ocean off Juan Fernández Islands and San Félix Island in the Desventuradas)

Minor morphometric differences among the species in 5a, 5b, and 5c (above) are evident in Figures 6–17 and Table 19.

Callanthias allporti Günther, 1876

Rosy Perch, Southern Splendid Perch, Southern Goldie, Allport's Groppo

Plate 1; Figures 1–5, 23; Tables 1–18, 20; Map 1

Callanthias allporti Günther, 1876:390 (original description; lectotype, herein designated BMNH 1875.11.12.38, 191 mm SL; type locality Tasmania).

Diagnosis. *Callanthias allporti* is distinguishable from all other species of *Callanthias* by the following combination of characters. Soft rays in both dorsal and anal fins almost always 10. Tubed lateral-line scales 36 to 47, usually 37 to 42. Secondary squamation usually present (Figure 5). Vomer almost always with few to several robust conical to caniniform teeth. Distinguishable by live coloration from *Callanthias australis,* which also occurs in the Australian–New Zealand region. *Callanthias allporti* has a single color phase and has a yellow chin, throat, and pectoral-fin base, whereas *C. australis* has a distinctive male color phase, lacks yellow on chin and throat, and has a red pectoral-fin base (Francis, 2012:97–99).

Description. Dorsal-fin rays XI, 10. Anal-fin rays III, 10 (rarely III, 9). Pectoral-fin rays 20 to 23 (usually 20–22). Caudal fin emarginate to lunate, often with long filamentous lobes in adults. Pseudobranch (Figure 4) with 20 to 30 filaments. Gillrakers 7 to 10 + 22 to 27—total 30 to 36. Sum of total number of gillrakers on first arch plus number of tubed lateral-line scales in individual specimens 66 to 81 (usually 68–76). Circum-caudal-peduncular scales 21 to 25. Scales between anal-fin origin and lateral line 15 to 20 (usually 17 or 18). Epineurals associated with first 10 to 14 vertebrae. Epurals 3 (very rarely 2). Lateral aspect of snout (usually) and lachrymal with scales. Gular region rarely with a few scales anteriorly. Membranes of dorsal, anal, pectoral, and pelvic fins without scales, but scales sometimes present at bases of fins; caudal fin well covered with scales for considerable distance out onto fin (in some specimens almost entire fin covered with scales). Frequency distributions for countable characters are given in Tables 2–17, and morphometric data for the four species of *Callanthias* (*allporti, legras,* *parini, ruber*) usually having 10 soft rays in both dorsal and anal fins are presented in Table 18.

Coloration. Günther (1876:391) noted "Uniform reddish (in spirits)," and Boulenger (1895:335, pl. XV) noted "Uniform reddish golden" and presented a fine black and white drawing of *C. allporti*. Kuiter (2004:11) wrote "Plain pink with a yellowish head and ventral fins." In the specimens in the five figures on p. 11 in Kuiter (2004) the irides of the eyes are mainly blue. Francis (2012:97) presented a photograph of *C. allporti* and wrote that the body is "pink with yellowish head, chin, throat, and pectoral fin base. Upper and lower tail lobes usually yellowish. . . . Eye iridescent blue." Roberts (1996:44) presented a photograph of a specimen of 170 mm SL (NMNZ P.32091), labeled "Southern Splendid Perch," with body and fins almost entirely reddish to red orange except for black distal band on soft dorsal fin and narrow black edging on distal border of middle of caudal fin.

Designation of lectotype. Günther (1876) based his description of *Callanthias allporti* on two specimens (BMNH 1875.11.12.38–39; 191 & 193 mm SL) but did not designate either of them as the type. To unequivocally fix the name of the species to a zoological entity, we hereby designate as the lectotype of *Callanthias allporti* Günther, 1876, the syntype of 191 mm SL (BMNH 1875.11.12.38). By that action the other syntype (BMNH 1875.11.12.39, 193 mm SL) becomes the paralectotype.

Dimorphism. There are two distinct morphs of *Callanthias allporti*—one with relatively short caudal-fin lobes (n = 9; 57.9–176 mm SL), the other with longer caudal-fin lobes (n = 16; 114–252 mm SL) (Table 20). In addition, length of the ultimate anal soft ray is almost dimorphic (Table 20). These differences may be sex related, but we lack the data needed to confirm this.

Ecology and ethology. Off New Zealand, *Callanthias allporti* is found on rocky reefs usually deeper than 25 meters, but it occurs in shallower waters in Fiordland on the southwestern corner of the South Island (Francis, 2012:97). It feeds on zooplankton above the bottom, forming small aggregations or mixing "with the more common butterflyfish *Caesioperca lepidoptera* when at shallower depths" (Kuiter, 2004:11). Francis (2012:97) noted that *C. allporti* schools with Butterfly Perch (an anthiine serranid, *Caesioperca lepidoptera*) "by day, presumably feeding on plankton," and retreats to "caves and crevices in the reef when disturbed and at night."

Distribution. *Callanthias allporti* is an inhabitant of the waters of the Australian–New Zealand region. McCulloch (1934:44), in noting its presence off New South Wales, wrote that it is "commonly taken by the trawlers in deep water"; Norman (1937:55) reported it as occurring off New South Wales, South Australia, and Tasmania and mentioned 11 specimens (21–90 mm) collected in 122 meters off Tasmania; and Graham (1940:425) described a large specimen (238 mm without caudal fin, 412 mm TL) obtained near Oamaru, Otago (South Island, New Zealand). Scott (1979:133) reported two specimens collected off the east coast of Tasmania, one of them (157 mm SL) from 140 meters; the other one (195 mm SL) has dorsal- and anal-fin soft ray counts of 11 each, more like the fin-ray counts of *C. australis* than those of *C. allporti*. Francis (2012, map on p. 97) showed this species as occurring off the northeast coast of the North Island and off most of the coast of the South Island of New Zealand and noted its occurrence off the Chatham and Snares islands. Aizawa and Matsuura (1990:256, fig. 194) reported this species from off North Cape, New Zealand, but the specimen (201 mm SL) illustrated and described appears to be *Callanthias australis*. We have examined specimens collected well east of the North Island, over the southern Kermadec Ridge and Chatham Rise, off South Island and Tasmania, and from Bass Strait in depths of 0 (0/15) to 659 meters.

Etymology. Named *Callanthias allporti* for Martin Allport (1830–1878), Tasmanian lawyer, who made extensive collections of fishes and sent specimens to Albert Günther at the British Museum (Saunders, 2012:110–111).

Material examined. Thirty-six specimens, 58–252 mm SL. **SOUTH PACIFIC,** well east of North Island, New Zealand: LACM 11241-8 (1 specimen: 168 mm SL). **SOUTH PACIFIC,** Southern Kermadec Ridge: NMNZ P.21413 (1: 191). **NEW ZEALAND,** Chatham Rise: NMNZ P.8391 (3: 139–196). **NEW ZEALAND,** South Island: HUMZ 66638–66641 (4: 196–216), KA 503A (1: 252), KA 513H (1: 245), NMNZ P.4268 (1: 155), NMNZ P.6572 (1: 208), NMNZ P.16297 (1: 176), NMNZ P.16837 (2: 179 & 184), NMNZ P.16870 (4: 118–151), NMNZ P.16872 (1: 133), NMNZ P.19906 (1: 124), NMNZ 20204 (1: 116), NMNZ P.21125 (5: 114–132). **NEW ZEALAND** (presumably, no data): NMNZ P.8135 (1: 226). **AUSTRALIA,** Bass Strait: AMS E.2987 (1: 129). **AUSTRALIA,** Tasmania: BMNH 1875.11.12.38 (lectotype: 191), BMNH 1875.11.12.39 (paralectotype: 193), BMNH 1937.9.21.26–27 (2: 58 & 67), NMV A3448 (2: 67 & 81).

Callanthias australis Ogilby, 1899

Northern Splendid Perch, Goldie, Glorious Groppo

Plate 2; Figures 1–13, 19, 20; Tables 1–17, 19, 20; Map 1

Callanthias platei australis Ogilby, 1899:173 (original description; lectotype, herein designated AMS I.3973, 166 mm SL; type locality off Norah Head [33°20' S, 151°41' E], 36 miles north of Port Jackson, New South Wales, Australia).

Callanthias australis Ogilby, 1899: combination used by many authors, including Anderson, 1999:2555 (species account).

Callanthias splendens Griffin, 1921:352, pl. 55, fig. 1 (original description; illustration; holotype AIM MA773, 183 mm SL; type locality entrance to Hauraki Gulf, Auckland, New Zealand).

Diagnosis. *Callanthias australis* is distinguishable from *allporti, legras, parini,* and *ruber* in almost always having 11 (very rarely 10 or 12) soft rays in both dorsal and anal fins, whereas the four aforementioned species have 10 in both fins (rarely 9 or 11). It is quite similar morphologically to the other two species in the genus, *japonicus* and *platei,* being essentially identical with them in countable characters and only very slightly different from them in a few morphometric traits (see Figures 6–13; Tables 1–17, 19). Secondary squamation usually present on head and body. Vomerine teeth, when present, small and conical; vomer often without teeth. Distinguishable by live coloration from *Callanthias allporti,* which also occurs in the Australian–New Zealand region. *Callanthias allporti* has a single color phase and a yellow chin, throat, and pectoral-fin base, whereas *C. australis* has a distinctive male color phase, lacks yellow on chin and throat, and has a red pectoral-fin base (Francis, 2012:97–99).

Description. Dorsal-fin rays XI, 11 (very rarely X, 12; XI, 10; or XI, 12). Anal-fin rays III, 11 (very rarely III, 10). Pectoral-fin rays 18 to 23 (usually 21 or 22). Caudal fin emarginate to almost truncate, larger individuals frequently with elongated lobes. Pseudobranch (Figure 4) with 11 to 43 filaments, tending to increase in number with growth (Figures 19, 20). Gillrakers 7 to 11 + 23 to 28—total 30 to 38 (usually 32–36).

Tubed lateral-line scales 31 to 42, usually 35 to 40, very rarely fewer than 34. Sum of total number of gillrakers on first arch plus number of tubed lateral-line scales in individual specimens 66 to 77 (usually 68–75). Circum-caudal-peduncular scales 21 to 25. Scales between anal-fin origin and lateral line 13 to 19. Epineurals associated with first 11 to 14 vertebrae. Epurals 3 (rarely 2). Anterodorsal and lateral aspects of snout usually with scales, lachrymal with scales. Gular region rarely with a few scales anteriorly. Membranes of dorsal and anal fins without scales; pectoral and pelvic fins scaly basally; caudal fin well covered with scales for considerable distance out onto fin. Frequency distributions for countable characters are given in Tables 2–17, and comparisons of morphometric data for the three species of *Callanthias* (*australis, japonicus, platei*), usually having 11 soft rays in both dorsal and anal fins, are presented in Table 19.

Coloration. Rivaton (1989, pl. 2) shows a specimen of *C. australis* with dull purplish head; anterodorsal part of body, dorsalmost and ventralmost portions of caudal peduncle, and fins, except caudal, bright yellow; most of body pallid; caudal fin dull yellow basally, remainder of caudal fin mostly purple, with produced upper and lower lobes yellowish. Roberts (1996:44) displays a photograph of a specimen of 250 mm SL (NMNZ P.29186), labeled "Northern Splendid Perch," with body and pectoral, pelvic, and caudal fins mostly purplish; stripe through eye, large spot on nape, spot at base of pectoral fin, caudal peduncle, middle of caudal fin, and dorsal and anal fins yellow.

"Juveniles pink with subtle mauve markings. Females yellow to orange or pink. Males variable with mood, sometimes showing almost white fins" (Kuiter, 2004:8). Two males in the photographs in Kuiter (2004:8, 9) are mostly red orange with some purple dorsal to the eye; head of a third male is mainly purple, and anterior half of body is mostly purple; one of the three males has dorsal and anal fins mainly yellow overlain with reddish and purple spots and markings and distal borders purple; the other two have dorsal and anal fins pink to orange. (On all three of those males the paired fins are mostly pink to orange, and the caudal fin is mainly purple with large central yellow splotch extending from base of fin almost to its distal border. A photograph of one of those males is reproduced in Roberts and Gomon, 2008:549.) A fourth male (Kuiter, 2004:9) with "unusual deep water colouration" has rosy to pale ground color on head, body, and fins with many red-orange spots on body and on basal portions of dorsal and anal fins; dull yellow spot ringed with red-orange near base of pectoral fin; large bright yellow splotch on posterior part of caudal peduncle that extends out onto middle of caudal fin; triangular-shaped area of red-orange enclosing peripheral stripe of yellow at distal end of each lobe of caudal fin. Doak (1972, pl. 9) has a color illustration (with two individuals labeled *Callanthias allporti*) that shows the usual and "deep-water" patterns of coloration displayed by males of *C. australis* as depicted in Kuiter (2004:8, 9), and Edgar et al. (1982:67) has a color plate with two examples (male above, juvenile below) of *C. australis* (labeled as *C. allporti*) in which the male shown resembles some of the individuals seen in Kuiter (2004:8, fig. D; 9, fig. H).

Francis (2012:98–99) presented a photograph depicting a male and female in close association and another showing a spawning male that resembles the male depicted in Kuiter (2004:9) that was described as having "unusual deep water colouration." Francis described the coloration of *C. australis* as

> Females uniformly pink-red. Males have deep mauve head and front of body, red rear body, yellow tail centre, and purple tail edges. Both sexes have a red pectoral fin base. Male's anal and dorsal fins yellow or brown with blue margins. During spawning, males are orange-red, covered in white lattice pattern; fins white with red or orange markings, and tail with red tips. (Francis 2012:99)

Francis added that *C. australis* differs from *C. allporti* "in having a distinctive male colour phase, in lacking a yellow chin and throat, and in having a red pectoral fin base" (Francis 2012:99).

Designation of lectotype. When he described *Callanthias platei australis,* Ogilby (1899) had three specimens at hand (AMS I. 3972, I. 3973, I. 3977; 162–166 mm SL) but failed to select one of them as the type. To firmly associate the name with a specimen, we designate AMS I. 3973 (166 mm SL) as the lectotype of *Callanthias australis.* The other syntypes become paralectotypes. The type specimens are three of six individuals reported by Waite (1899:80) as having been caught by trawl off Norah Head (36 miles north of Port Jackson), New South Wales; the disposition of the other three is unknown. Ogilby (1899:172) obtained a specimen of this species in the Sydney Market in November 1897, well before examining those caught off Norah Head, but it is not clear whether he considered it when describing *C. australis.*

Callanthias splendens. Griffin (1921:352, pl. 55, fig. 1) described and illustrated *Callanthias splendens* from a single specimen (AIM MA773,

183 mm SL) collected at the entrance to Hauraki Gulf, Auckland, New Zealand. Comparisons of the holotype of *C. splendens* directly with the lectotype (AMS I. 3973, 166 mm SL) and two paralectotypes (AMS I. 3972, 162 mm SL, & I. 3977, 163 mm SL) of *C. australis* showed that the holotype has much more secondary squamation than do the types of *C. australis* and that the holotype lacks vomerine and palatine dentition, whereas the vomerine and palatine teeth are small but in well-defined patches/bands in the types of *C. australis.* Secondary squamation and vomerine dentition show much variation in *C. australis,* and the findings for the holotype of *C. splendens* are well within the ranges of variation found in those characters in other specimens of this species. In addition, data recorded for the many counts and measurements made on the holotype agree well with those from the types of *C. australis* and with data taken from the other specimens of *C. australis* examined, leaving no doubt that *Callanthias splendens* Griffin, 1921, is a junior synonym of *Callanthias australis* Ogilby, 1899.

Sexual dichromatism and dimorphism. As noted above under **Coloration,** sexual dichromatism is present. *Callanthias australis* has two distinct morphs—one with relatively short caudal-fin lobes (n = 53; 41.1–217 mm SL), the other with longer caudal-fin lobes (n = 3; 171–227 mm SL) (Table 20). These differences are likely sex related, but we lack the data needed to confirm this.

Further, as can be seen in Table 20, *C. australis* can be placed in three different groups based on lengths of caudal-fin lobes: short caudal-fin lobes (n = 39; 41.1–217 mm SL), medium-length caudal-fin lobes (n = 14; 69.0–211 mm SL), and long caudal-fin lobes (n = 3; 171–227 mm SL). Assuming that *C. australis* is protogynous, as appears likely, the group with medium-length caudal-fin lobes may consist of transitional individuals that were undergoing sex change at the time of capture.

Reproduction. Eggs have not been described (Trnski and Miskiewicz, 1998:190). Francis (2012:99) reported that "School spawning has been observed in August and October: several males with their dorsal and anal fins raised spiral around one or two females; the group then swims upwards for several metres, releasing eggs and sperm at the peak of their movement."

Early life history. Trnski and Miskiewicz (1998:189–191) described the early larvae of *Callanthias australis,* illustrating (fig. 54) four specimens (2.8–6.7 mm). Miskiewicz et al. (2000:280–284, fig. 64) also provided a description of the larvae, using the illustrations that appeared in Trnski and Miskiewicz (1998). Larvae have been collected from inshore and offshore waters off Sydney, both near the surface and in midwater, being most abundant in midwater (Gray and Miskiewicz, 2000:562).

Ecological notes. According to Trnski and Miskiewicz (1998:190), this species occurs in coastal waters on rocky reefs at depths of 20 to 200 meters. Kuiter (2004:8) noted that C. *australis* occurs on offshore reefs and off islands, usually at depths greater than 25 meters, and is "often abundant on reefs that level out at 50 m." Francis (2012:99) stated that this species feeds on plankton (especially crustaceans) and is found on rocky reefs mainly off coastal headlands and offshore islands, usually in waters deeper than 25 meters; customarily it occurs near the bottom, often close to a reef/sand boundary.

Ethology. *Callanthias australis* often schools with the anthiine serranids *Caesioperca lepidoptera* and *Caprodon longimanus,* retreating to caves or crevices at night and when disturbed; as a consequence, individuals of this species are "easily overlooked by divers" (Francis, 2012:99).

Doak (1972:31) reported the prespawning behavior of this species (misidentified as *Callanthias allporti*) in New Zealand waters. In 180 feet (55 meters) of water he observed about 30 members of this species rising and then sinking close to the bottom. A number of individuals showed a beautiful latticework pattern with widespread gaudy fins; some of these were pairing with smaller individuals with less attractive coloration. Those with the latticework were males, and the plainer ones were females, in even numbers.

> Often a female was seen just above or below a male as he pirouetted around her displaying his dorsal and anal fins to make his body appear a third greater in depth. At times two or three males would meet in an aggressive display, twisting and turning around one another as each fish demonstrated his virility and majesty with threatening gestures, his body taut and curving. Our time at this depth was too limited to determine whether this was an actual spawning or preliminary "dance."

Etymology. The word "australis," Latin for "southern," is an apt appellation for a species known only from the Australian–New Zealand region.

Distribution. The type specimens of this species were obtained from Port Jackson, New South Wales (Ogilby, 1899:172). Later Waite (1899:80) reported six specimens (as *Callanthias platei,* three of which are part of the type series for *Callanthias australis*) collected off Norah Head (36 miles north of Port Jackson), New South Wales, in 32 to 48 fathoms (59–88 meters). Much later Rivaton (1989:152) recounted finding it in the Chesterfield Islands region of the Coral Sea, and Trnski and Miskiewicz (1998:190) noted that it is found off southern Australia from Shark Bay, Western Australia, to Port Macquarie, New South Wales, including Tasmania, and also occurs off New Zealand. Francis (2012, map, p. 99) showed that it is found off most of the coast of the North Island and off the northern coast of the South Island of New Zealand and mentioned its presence off the Kermadec and Three Kings islands. Aizawa and Matsuura (1990:256, fig. 194) reported *Callanthias allporti* from off North Cape, New Zealand, but the specimen (201 mm SL) illustrated and described appears to be *Callanthias australis.* We have examined specimens collected over Wanganella Bank (Norfolk Ridge), off New Zealand's North and South islands, from the Coral Sea, and off the Australian states of Queensland, New South Wales, Victoria, Tasmania, South Australia, and Western Australia in depths of 15 to 366 (183/366) meters.

Material examined. One hundred and seven specimens, 22 to 227 mm SL **SOUTH PACIFIC,** Wanganella Bank, Norfolk Ridge: NMNZ P.21405 (1 specimen: 185 mm SL). **NEW ZEALAND,** North Island: ANSP 113342 (1: 189), AIM MA773 (holotype of *Callanthias splendens:* 183). **NEW ZEALAND,** Poor Knights Islands: NMNZ P.5337 (1: 169). **NEW ZEALAND,** South Island: GMBL 83-50 (1: 188). **CORAL SEA,** between New Caledonia and Queensland, GMBL 84-112 (1: 171). **QUEENSLAND:** QM I.21521 (1: 227). **NEW SOUTH WALES:** AMS I. 3972 (paralectotype: 162), AMS I. 3973 (lectotype: 166), AMS I. 3977 (paralectotype: 163), AMS IB 4332 (1: 217), AMS I. 12131 (1: 114), AMS I. 18624-001 (2: 34 & 38), AMS I. 19662-001 (2: 69 & 76), AMS I. 30421-003 (1: 207), GMBL 80-385 (2: 211 & 218), LACM 42624-5 (10: 61–137), NMNZ P.17279 (1: 97), USNM 177072 (2: 204 & 216), WAM P.25200-001 (4: 83–142), WAM P.25200-002 (4: 170–198), WAM P.25200-003 (5: 166–215), WAM P.27089-007 (1: 22), WAM P.27101-001 (1: 27), ZMUC CN. 2 (1: 151). **VICTORIA:** AMS E. 2183 (1: 191), AMS E. 2185 (1: 188), AMS IB 4615 (1: 209), NMV R11541 (1: 204), ZMUC CN 1 & 3 (2: 102 & 208). **VICTORIA/TASMANIA,** eastern edge of Bass Strait: AMS E. 3019 (1: 166), AMS E. 3020 (1: 158). **TASMANIA,** east coast of Flinders Island:

NMV A7926 (3: 170–183). **SOUTH AUSTRALIA/WESTERN AUSTRALIA,** Great Australian Bight: WAM P.26807-001 (1: 70). **WESTERN AUSTRALIA:** AMS E. 2365 (6: 69–141), AMS E. 2434 (12: 51–88), AMS I. 18709-002 (5: 90–133), AMS I. 20243-003 (1: 129), AMS I. 20244-002 (1: 132), AMS I. 31186001 (7: 30–49), CSIRO H. 2610-01 (1: 198), CSIRO H. 2610-03 (1: 187), CSIRO H. 2610-12 (1: 196), CSIRO H. 2610-13 (1: 170), CSIRO H. 2610-14 (1: 165), CSIRO H. 2610-15 (1: 141), CSIRO H. 2610-16 (5: 91–114), WAM P.23344-001 (1: 31), WAM P.27211-005 (1: 41), WAM P.27215-005 (1: 196), WAM P.28208-001 (1: 126).

Callanthias japonicus Franz, 1910

Japanese Splendid Perch, Japanese Goldie, Petunia Groppo

Plate 3; Figures 1–9, 14–17, 19, 21; Tables 1–17, 19, 20; Map 2

Callanthias japonicus Franz, 1910:40, pl. 6, fig. 49 (original description; illustration; holotype ZSM [old collection] destroyed in World War II; type locality Aburatsubo, Sagami Sea, Japan).

Diagnosis. *Callanthias japonicus* is distinguishable from *allporti, legras, parini,* and *ruber* in having 11 soft rays in the dorsal fin and almost always 11 in the anal fin, whereas the four aforementioned species have 10 in both fins (rarely 9 or 11). It is quite similar morphologically to the other two species in the genus, *australis* and *platei,* showing only very minor differences from them in meristic and morphometric traits (see Figures 6–9, 14–17; Tables 1–17, 19). Secondary squamation well developed, usually present on head and body, frequently better developed posteriorly. Vomerine teeth usually very small.

Description. Dorsal-fin rays XI, 11. Anal-fin rays III, 11 (rarely III, 10). Pectoral-fin rays 20 to 22 (usually 21). Caudal fin emarginate to almost truncate, larger individuals frequently with elongated lobes. Pseudobranch (Figure 4) with 24 to 37 (usually 27–32) filaments, tending to increase in number with growth. Gillrakers 7 to 9 + 21 to 25—total 29 to 33 (usually 30–33). Tubed lateral-line scales 33 to 41 (usually 35–39). Sum of total number of gillrakers on first arch plus number of tubed lateral-line scales in individual specimens 65 to 73 (usually 67–70). Circum-caudal-peduncular scales 22 to 25. Scales between anal-fin origin and lateral line 15 to 18. Epineurals associated with first 12 to 14 vertebrae. Epurals 3. Lateral aspect of snout (usually) and lachrymal with scales. Gular region rarely with a few scales anteriorly. Membranes of dorsal and anal fins without scales; pectoral, pelvic, and caudal fins scaly basally. Frequency distributions for countable characters are given in Tables 2–17, and comparisons of morphometric data for the three species of *Callanthias* (*australis, japonicus, platei*) usually having 11 soft rays in both dorsal and anal fins are presented in Table 19.

Coloration. Katayama (1984, pl. 124-E: same as pl. 51-L in Masuda et al., 1975) presented a photograph (by H. Masuda) of *C. japonicus* that depicts an individual with body and dorsum of head mostly orange; iris of eye, ventral part of head, dorsal and anal fins, and most of caudal fin bright yellow. A photograph in Yamakawa (1985, pl. 246) depicts a specimen (180 mm SL) with coloration similar to that in Katayama (1984), except dorsal half of body and dorsum of head with much red, ventral part of head mainly silvery, and middle of caudal fin yellow bordered by rose and lavender. Lee (1989:154, fig. 1) included a color photograph of a large specimen (ASIZP 056326, 233 mm SL; subsequently examined by CCB) that was described when fresh as

> reddish pink, yellowish ventrally. Dorsal and anal fins yellowish with purplish margins. Pectoral fin reddish pink with yellowish base. Ventral fin reddish pink. Caudal fin yellowish with pinkish outer edges, filaments bright yellowish.

Kuiter (2004:10) wrote "Pink to orange yellow with yellow to orange fins" and included three color photographs of this species, two males and one female (lengths ca. 22–25 cm), made at the Tokai Aquarium, Japan. Those individuals are mostly orange, but one male has much yellow ventrally, anterior to anal fin, that reaches to orbital region. The female is lavender and silvery along ventral portion of body. Dorsal and anal fins of males with borders of violet; those fins mostly yellow in female. Caudal fin of all three mostly violet to purple with broad bar of orange, dull yellow, or bright yellow at base of fin. Irides of eyes mostly bright yellow.

Sexual dichromatism and dimorphism. As noted above under **Coloration,** there are minor differences in pigmentation between the sexes. *Callanthias japonicus* has two distinct morphs—one with relatively short caudal-fin lobes (n = 17; 113–184 mm SL), the other with longer caudal-fin lobes (n = 7; 153–233 mm SL). The base of the anal fin tends to be shorter in specimens with short caudal-fin lobes and longer in those with longer lobes (Table 20). These differences may be sex related, but we lack data supporting this speculation.

Early life history. Okiyama (1988:419–421) described several larvae of *C. japonicus* and illustrated three (3.7 mm, 5.4 mm, 10.3 mm).

Ecology and ethology. *Callanthias japonicus* is found over "Deep rocky reefs, usually in excess of 60 m"; occurs in small groups when feeding on zooplankton in open water; and frequently accompanies other feeding planktivores, particularly species of the serranid subfamily Anthiinae (Kuiter, 2004:10).

Remarks. Kuiter (2004:10) mentioned that a population observed off northwestern Australia appears to be *C. japonicus*. We have seen no specimens of *Callanthias* from that region. In view of the close similarity of *C. japonicus* to *C. australis*, we think it more likely that the northwestern Australian population is *C. australis*.

Distribution. *Callanthias japonicus* has been reported from southern Korea, Sea of Japan, Sagami Sea, Suruga Bay, southern Japan, Ryukyu Islands, East China Sea, Taiwan, Okinawa Trough, and Emperor Seamounts (Katayama, 1960a:167; Katayama, 1984:138; Lee, 1989:154; Lindberg and Krasyukova, 1969:54–56; Masuda et al., 1975:221; Mundy, 2005:350; Nakabo, 2002:732; Schmidt, 1931:60; Senou et al., 2006:449; Shinohara and Matsuura, 1997:303; Shinohara et al., 2001:322; Shinohara et al., 2005:431; Shinohara et al., 2011:49; Yamakawa, 1985:467, 667). More specifically, within the system known as the Emperor Seamounts, Mundy (2005:350) noted its occurrence at Milwaukee and Koko seamounts based on Novikov et al. (1981). (**Caveat:** Bruce Mundy, who compiled a checklist of Hawaiian fishes [Mundy, 2005], wrote to WDA [03 September 2013] that "The records of *Callanthias japonicus* from the Emperor Seamounts need verification. The Hawaii Undersea Research Laboratory re-examined its images of fish in the Hawaiian Islands that were identified as *Callanthias* and found that all were misidentified *Grammatonotus* species. The early Russian Emperor Seamount records of *Callanthias* may also be misidentified *Grammatonotus*.") The only specimens that we examined were collected off Japan and Taiwan; depth data are known for only one of those collections (120 meters); most specimens examined were obtained from markets.

Etymology. The name *japonicus*, Latinized version of "Japan," refers to the type locality of the species.

Material examined. Twenty-eight specimens, 113–233 mm SL. **JAPAN:** FMNH 89235 (1 specimen: 182 mm SL), FMNH 91772 (1: 189), FUMT P. 1372 (1: 185), FUMT 1373 & 1374 (2: both 180), HUMZ 51969 (1: 185), Katayama's No. 3998 (1: 165), NSMT-P 22378 (1: 166), ZUMT 23854 (1: 149), ZUMT 39190–39198 (9: 125–162), ZUMT 48073–48076 (4: 176–184), ZUMT 51007 (1: 138), ZUMT 51713–51715 (3: 113–153), ZUMT 56153 (1: 158). **TAIWAN:** ASIZP 0056326 (1: 233).

Callanthias legras Smith, 1948

African Splendid Perch, African Goldie

Plate 4; Figures 1–5, 22; Tables 1–18, 20; Map 3

Callanthias legras Smith, 1948:335, fig. 1 (original description; illustration; holotype SAIAB 30, 169 mm SL; type locality off Algoa Bay, South Africa, in 30 fathoms [55 meters]).

Diagnosis. *Callanthias legras* is distinguishable from all other species of *Callanthias* by the following combination of characters. Soft rays in both dorsal and anal fins almost always 10. Tubed lateral-line scales 28 to 36, usually 29 to 33. Circum-caudal-peduncular scales 15 to 17. Secondary squamation usually absent. Vomer usually with few to several robust conical to caniniform teeth. Epurals 2, very rarely 3.

Description. Dorsal-fin rays XI, 10 (rarely X, 11; XI, 9; or XII, 10). Anal-fin rays III, 10 (rarely III, 9 or III, 11). Pectoral-fin rays 18 to 21 (usually 19 or 20). Caudal fin emarginate to almost truncate, upper and lower lobes may be slightly produced. Pseudobranch (Figure 4) with 19 to 28 (usually 20–24) filaments, showing slight tendency to increase in number with growth. Gillrakers 9 to 11 + 22 to 27—total 31 to 38 (usually 32–36). Sum of total number of gillrakers on first arch plus number of tubed lateral-line scales in individual specimens 60 to 70 (usually 62–68). Scales between anal-fin origin and lateral line 12 to 14. Epineurals associated with first 13 to 16 vertebrae. Anterodorsal part of snout with or without scales, rest of dorsum of snout almost always with scales, lateral aspect of snout usually without scales, lachrymal usually with scales, anterior part of gular region usually with scales. Scales present proximally on dorsal and anal fins; pectoral, pelvic, and caudal fins scaly basally. Frequency distributions for countable characters are given in Tables 2–17, and comparisons of morphometric data for the four species of *Callanthias* (*allporti, legras, parini, ruber*) usually having 10 soft rays in both dorsal and anal fins are presented in Table 18.

Coloration. "Like its congeners, colours are a mix of orange and yellow, but the ventral fins are conspicuously white" (Kuiter, 2004:7). The photograph of *C. legras* in Kuiter (2004:7) shows a specimen with upper body and dorsum of head mostly orange, with bright yellow band from snout running around eye to continue along length of body where it merges with yellow of caudal fin; ventral to yellow band a lavender band running from snout almost to base of caudal fin; ventral to lavender band a yellow band running from base of pelvic fin to base of caudal fin; iris of eye yellow adjacent to pupil with lavender to violet peripherally; dorsal, anal, and caudal fins mainly bright yellow, last few rays of dorsal fin orange, last few rays of anal fin red, dorsalmost and ventralmost principal rays of caudal fin orange to red proximally, lavender distally; pectoral fin mostly yellow with considerable lavender at base ventrally; pelvic fin strikingly white.

Dimorphism. *Callanthias legras* has two distinct morphs—one with a relatively short anal fin (n = 14; 90.2–170 mm SL), the other with a longer anal fin (n = 22; 100–202 mm SL). The penultimate dorsal and anal soft rays and lower caudal-fin lobe tend to be shorter in specimens with a short anal fin and longer in those with a longer fin (Table 20). The 169-mm-SL female noted in the next section has a relatively short anal fin (40.3% SL) and short penultimate anal soft ray (ca. 11% SL), whereas the 175-mm-SL male mentioned below has a considerably longer anal fin (47.6% SL) and longer penultimate anal soft ray (14.9% SL). These differences in anal-fin morphology appear to be sex related.

Sexuality and reproduction. The gonads of two specimens (SAIAB 40768) were examined histologically by William A. Roumillat. He found one specimen (169 mm SL) to have been a spawning (or immediately postspawning) female with well-developed prespawning oocytes and a considerable amount of oocytic atresia; the other, a male (175 mm SL), was preparing to spawn and had residual oocytes throughout the testes. Those data suggest that *Callanthias legras* may be a protogynous hermaphrodite, and because the specimens were collected in mid-September, spawning probably begins in the latter part of the austral winter.

Ecological note. "Occurs over rocky bottoms to a depth of about 400 m" (Kuiter, 2004:7).

Distribution. *Callanthias legras* has been reported from off South Africa (in the southeastern Atlantic and southwestern Indian Ocean; J. L. B. Smith, 1948:336, 1955:345, 1961: 361; M. M. Smith, 1980:177; Heemstra and Anderson, 1986:538–539) and Namibia (Allué et al., 2000:108; all of the Namibian localities given by Allué et al., 2000, for this species are off the Northern Cape Province of South Africa). The specimens we examined were collected in the southwestern Indian Ocean and southeastern Atlantic off South Africa (east, south, and west coasts, from KwaZulu-Natal to the Northern Cape Province) in depths of 55 to 245 meters.

Etymology. "Named for Mr. M. G. le Gras, of Port Elizabeth, who has collected many valuable fishes" (Smith, 1948:337).

Material examined. Forty-six specimens, 90–202 mm SL. **SOUTH AFRICA,** east coast: SAIAB 7820 (1 specimen: 157 mm SL). **SOUTH AFRICA,** south coast: GMBL 92–1 (3: 139–150), GMBL 92–2 (6: 94–160), SAIAB 30 (holotype: 169), SAIAB 2740 (1: 168), SAIAB 28355 (1: 170), SAIAB 28356 (1: 177), SAIAB 30330 (2: 172 & 173), SAIAB 38213 (1: 119), SAIAB 38422 (6: 138–197), SAIAB 38925 (1: 155), SAIAB 38926 (6: 99–162), SAIAB 40768 (2: 169 & 175), SAM 21494 (1: 144), SAM 24705 (1: 164), SAM 25022 (6: 130–193), USNM 395020 (2: 123 & 147). **SOUTH AFRICA,** west coast: IIPB 63/1985 (1: 202), IIPB 64/1985 (1: 197), IIPB 65/1985 (1: 184). **SOUTH AFRICA,** exact locality unknown: SAIAB 7821 (1: 90).

Callanthias parini Anderson and Johnson, 1984

Nazca Splendid Perch, Parin's Groppo

Plate 5; Figures 1–5, 18, 23; Tables 1–18, 20; Map 4

Callanthias sp., Parin et al., 1981:14 (brief description of material collected by R/V IKHTIANDR on the Nazca Ridge).

Callanthias parini Anderson and Johnson, 1984:943, figs. 1 and 2 (original description; illustrations; holotype USNM 265444, 175 mm SL; type locality Nazca Ridge at 21°25' S, 81°37' W in 325 meters).

Diagnosis. *Callanthias parini* is distinguishable from all other species of *Callanthias* by the following combination of characters. Soft rays in both dorsal and anal fins 10. Tubed lateral-line scales 24 to 31, usually 26 to 29. Circum-caudal-peduncular scales 21 to 24 (usually 23 or 24). Secondary squamation poorly developed. Vomerine teeth small.

Description. Dorsal-fin rays XI, 10. Anal-fin rays III, 10. Pectoral-fin rays 20 to 22 (rarely 20). Caudal fin lunate with dorsal and ventral lobes produced in larger specimens. Pseudobranch (Figure 4) with 20 to 27 (usually 23 or 24) filaments. Gillrakers 8 to 10 + 21 to 24—total 29 to 34 (usually 31–33). Sum of total number of gillrakers on first arch plus number of tubed lateral-line scales in individual specimens 55 to 63 (usually 58–60). Scales between anal-fin origin and lateral line 14 to 19. Epineurals associated with first 10 to 12 vertebrae. Epurals 3 (occasionally 2). Small section on lateral aspect of snout without scales, lachrymal with scales, gular region without scales. Membranes of dorsal and anal fins without scales; pectoral, pelvic, and caudal fins scaly basally. Frequency distributions for countable characters are given in Tables 2–17, and comparisons of morphometric data for the four species of *Callanthias* (*allporti, legras, parini, ruber*) usually having 10 soft rays in both dorsal and anal fins are presented in Table 18.

Coloration. Anderson and Johnson (1984:948) described the coloration of a specimen in a transparency received from N. V. Parin as "head and body mostly orange; iris mostly pale anterodorsally and mostly melanistic elsewhere; dorsal and anal fins yellow-orange; pectoral and pelvic fins orange; caudal fin dull orange." The image in that transparency is reproduced here in Plate 5.

Sexuality and sexual dimorphism. Anderson and Johnson (1984:948) wrote: "Our specimens are separable into distinct morphs based on lengths of dorsal-, anal-, and caudal-fin rays. . . . Individuals less than about 160 mm SL have short fin rays and larger specimens have long fin rays." William A. Roumillat examined histological sections of the gonads of ten specimens (148–179 mm SL), but because the viscera were poorly preserved, sex could not be determined unequivocally for each specimen. Despite this, it appears that the two morphs represent different sexual stages of what is likely a protogynous species (see Anderson and Johnson, 1984:945, table 2, and Table 20 herein).

Ecological note. Parin et al. (1997:195) noted that all of the food found in stomachs of *C. parini* was of pelagic origin, predominantly plankton.

Length/weight relationships. N. V. Parin provided us with data on standard length (mm) and weight (grams) for 26 specimens (125–193 mm SL) of *C. parini.* Those specimens were collected by A. N. Kotlyar and N. B. Maksimov on 14 February 1983 aboard the R/V PROFESSOR MESYATZEV at a station on the Nazca Ridge, near Ecliptic Seamount (Lat. 22°06' S, Long. 81°18' W, in 225 meters of water). In Figure 18 specimen data are plotted and the equation for the length/weight relationship is presented.

Distribution. Parin and his associates (Parin, 1990, 1991; Parin et al., 1981, 1997) noted the presence of *C. parini* on the Nazca and Sala y Gómez submarine ridges in depths of 230 to 350 meters. All specimens we examined were collected over those ridges in depths of 210 (210–230) to 340 meters.

Etymology. Named for Nikolai Vasil'evich Parin (1932–2012), who during his many years as an ichthyologist with the P. P. Shirshov Institute of Oceanology, Russian Academy of Sciences, Moscow, made many very important contributions to the study of fishes, not the least of which was providing material for many other scientists. All of the specimens of *C. parini* that we examined were received from Parin. Collette (2013) provided an obituary for Parin.

Material examined. Nineteen specimens, 40–179 mm SL. **NAZCA RIDGE:** ANSP 152995 (1 specimen: 153 mm SL), BPBM 29399 (1: 148), CAS 54643 (1: 179), USNM 265444 (holotype: 175), USNM 395064 (1: 177), USNM 395065 (1: 164), USNM 395066 (2: 163 & 168), USNM 395068 (1: 68), USNM 395069 (1: 40), USNM 395070 (6: 143–168), ZMMU P-15572 (2: 157 & 174). **SALA Y GÓMEZ RIDGE:** USNM 395067 (1: 95).

Callanthias platei Steindachner, 1898

Juan Fernández Splendid Perch, San Félix Groppo

Plate 6; Figures 1–5, 10–17, 20, 21; Tables 1–17, 19, 20; Map 4

Callanthias platei Steindachner 1898:284, pl. 15 (original description; illustration; lectotype, herein designated ZMB 15624, 182 mm SL; type locality Juan Fernández Islands).

Diagnosis. *Callanthias platei* is distinguishable from *allporti, legras, parini,* and *ruber* in having 11 soft rays in the dorsal fin and almost always 11 in the anal fin, whereas the four aforementioned species have 10 in both fins (rarely 9 or 11). It is quite similar morphologically to the other two species in the genus, *australis* and *japonicus,* showing only very minor differences from them in meristic and morphometric traits (see Figures 10–17; Tables 1–17, 19, 20). Secondary squamation well developed on head and body (Figure 5). Vomerine teeth small to minute.

Description. Dorsal-fin rays XI, 11. Anal-fin rays III, 11 (rarely III, 12). Pectoral-fin rays 20 to 22 (usually 21). Caudal fin lunate to forked, some larger individuals with outermost dorsal and ventral rays considerably produced. Pseudobranch (Figure 4) with 21 to 36 filaments, tending to increase in number with growth. Gillrakers 8 or 9 + 23 to 26—total 31 to 35 (usually 31–33). Tubed lateral-line scales 36 to 42 (usually 37–41). Sum of total number of gillrakers on first arch plus number of tubed lateral-line scales in individual specimens 69 to 76 (usually 71–73). Circum-caudal-peduncular scales 22 to 25 (usually 23 or 24). Scales between anal-fin origin and lateral line 14 to 17 (usually 15 or 16). Epineurals associated with first 12 or 13 vertebrae. Epurals 3 (rarely 2). Lateral aspect of snout and lachrymal with scales, gular region without scales. Frequency distributions for countable characters are given in Tables 2–17, and comparisons of morphometric data for the three species of *Callanthias* (*australis, japonicus, platei*) usually having 11 soft rays in both dorsal and anal fins are presented in Table 19.

Coloration. In describing the coloration of *Callanthias platei,* Steindachner (1898:286) wrote:

Obere Kopfhälfte bräunlich rosenroth oder blass röthlichviolett, untere weisslich, metallisch glänzend, ein Silberstreif trennt zuweilen beide Hälften scharf von einander und endigt vorne am Seitenrande der Schnauze, hinten am untern Deckelstachel. Seiten des Rumpfes tief hinab rosenroth mit bräunlichem Striche. Bauchseite und unterster Theil der Körperseiten silberweiss mit stahlblauem Schimmer (bei Weingeistexemplaren). . . .

Ueber das natürliche Aussehen dieses Fisches schreibt Dr. PLATE: Der ganze Körper ist wunderschön rosa-violett gefärbt. Die Rücken- und Afterflossen sind dunkelroth. An der Bauchseite wird die Rosafarbe des Körpers etwas blasser und nimmt etwas Silberschimmer an. An der Schwanzflosse überwiegt bald der rothe, bald der violette Farbenton. Iris schwärzlich.

[Upper half of head brownish rosy red or pale reddish violet, lower half whitish with metallic shine, silver stripe distinctly separating halves from each other and terminating in front on side of snout, in rear below lower spine of operculum. Sides of body deep rosy red with brownish lines. Sides of abdomen and undersides silver white with steel blue luster (in alcohol specimens). . . .

On natural coloration of these fishes Dr. Plate wrote: Entire body colored an exquisite rose-violet. Back and posterior fins dark red. On side of abdomen rose color somewhat paler taking on slightly silver luster. Caudal fin predominantly red and violet. Iris blackish.]

Kuiter (2004:10) wrote that females are mostly orange, males mauve, and presented three color illustrations of specimens (about 20–28 cm in length) photographed at a depth of about 25 meters off Robinson Crusoe Island (Juan Fernández Islands). One photograph shows an individual (apparently a male) that is mainly various shades of purple except for orange band extending along ventral part of body from anterior end of anal-fin base to just beyond base of caudal fin. Another one portrays an individual (apparently a female) with much orange and lavender on head, body with lavender ground color overlain with specks of orange and yellow anteriorly, posteriorly body mainly yellow, caudal fin bright yellow except for base, which is dull orange dorsally and ventrally. Iris of eye of each of those two specimens with much yellow framed by deep blue dorsally and ventrally.

Designation of lectotype. According to Steindachner (1898:284), the original description of *Callanthias platei* was based on five specimens

(15.7–24 cm in length, presumably total length). At the Museum für Naturkunde, Humboldt-Universität zu Berlin, there are nine specimens (ZMB 15623 & 15624, 118–189 mm SL) that are considered to be syntypes. (There is confusion here because the catalogue entry for the syntypes indicates that there are/were 11 specimens [Peter Bartsch, *in litt.* to GDJ, 28 October 2013]). In order to firmly associate the name of the species with a specimen, we designate a 182-mm SL specimen in ZMB 15624 as the lectotype of *Callanthias platei* Steindachner, 1898. The other specimens formerly catalogued as ZMB 15624 have been assigned a new catalogue number: ZMB 34739; they along with the syntypes catalogued as ZMB 15623 become paralectotypes.

Dimorphism. The specimens of *C. platei* that we examined fall into two groups—those with short caudal-fin lobes (n = 18; 70.5–182 mm SL) and those with long caudal-fin lobes (n= 8; 137–192 mm SL) (Table 20). The differences between the groups may be sex related, but we lack data that would support or refute this.

Ecology and ethology. Kuiter (2004:10) noted: "Usually seen at depths over 25 m, near large caves and overhangs. Swims in open water when feeding on zooplankton, often in schools mixed with" *Caprodon* (an anthiine serranid).

According to Ogilby (1899:174), Plate wrote "of the eastern Pacific form [*C. platei*] that it arrives at the island [Juan Fernández] at rare and irregular intervals in vast shoals consisting of many hundreds of individuals, and states that he has seen such swarms of fishes that they seemed to form a solid mass beneath the surface of the water, showing like golden spots in the remoter distance."

Distribution. *Callanthias platei* has been reported from the southeastern Pacific off the Desventuradas and Juan Fernández islands (Rendahl, 1921:55; Sepúlveda and Pequeño, 1985:88; Sepúlveda, 1987:241, 242; Pequeño, 1989:59; Meléndez and Villalba, 1992:10; Pequeño and Lamilla, 2000:434; Pequeño and Sáez, 2000:31; and Dyer and Westneat, 2010:592, 595, 598, 605, 607). We examined specimens collected off San Félix Island (in the Desventuradas) and off the Juan Fernández Islands in depths of 0 (0–20) to 165 (140–165) meters.

Miscellaneous. "Das Fleisch ist schmackhaft" (The flesh is tasty) (Steindachner, 1898:286).

Etymology. *Callanthias platei* was named for Ludwig Hermann Plate (1862–1937), German biologist who became professor of zoology and director of the Phyletische Museum at Jena and made a number of expeditions, including one (1893–1896) to South America (Robinson, 2008). The material Steindachner used in preparing his description of *Callanthias platei* was obtained by Plate from the Juan Fernández Islands (Steindachner, 1898).

Material examined. Twenty-six specimens, 70–192 mm SL. **SAN FÉLIX ISLAND:** SIO 65–629 (5 specimens: 70–148 mm SL), USNM 307594 (1: 92). **JUAN FERNÁNDEZ ISLANDS:** BMNH 1935.9.10.3–4 (1 of 2: 168), CAS 24145 (2: 129 & 160), MCZ 46163 (6: 106–192), MCZ 52518 (6: 124–181), ZMB 15623 (2 paralectotypes: 170 & 176), ZMB 15624 (lectotype: 182), ZMB 34739 (2 paralectotypes: 118 & 123).

Callanthias ruber (Rafinesque, 1810)

Bird-of-Paradise Fish, Parrot Seaperch, Matulic Silioglavac, Papagaio, Eastern Atlantic Groppo

Plate 7; Figures 1–5, 22; Tables 1–18, 20; Map 3

Lepimphis ruber Rafinesque, 1810:34, pl. 10, fig. 2 (original description, illustration; no types known; Mediterranean Sea, off Palermo, Sicily).

Bodianus peloritanus Cocco, 1829:142 (original description; no types known; Mediterranean Sea, off Messina, Sicily).

Anthias buphthalmos Bonaparte, 1833:fasc. 2 (original description, illustration; syntypes ANSP 13624–13636 [13: 74–101 mm SL], 17161 [1, dry skin, missing]; type locality western Mediterranean Sea).

Callanthias paradisaeus Lowe, 1839:76 (original description; holotype: BMNH 1855.11.29.13, 118 mm SL; type locality off Madeira). Lowe, 1843:13–18, pl. 3 (description, illustration).

Callanthias ruber (Rafinesque, 1810): Anderson, in press (brief description).

Diagnosis. *Callanthias ruber* is distinguishable from all other species of *Callanthias* by the following combination of characters. Soft rays in both dorsal and anal fins almost always 10. Tubed lateral-line scales 21 to 26, usually 22 to 25. Circum-caudal-peduncular scales 18 to 21, usually 20. Secondary squamation absent to poorly developed. Vomer with minute to moderate-sized conical teeth, teeth sometimes absent.

Description. Dorsal-fin rays XI, 10 (rarely X, 10; XI, 11; or XII, 10). Anal-fin rays III, 10 (rarely III, 11). Pectoral-fin rays 17 to 22, usually 20 or 21. Caudal fin lunate; individuals more than about 130 mm SL with long filamentous lobes. Pseudobranch (Figure 4) with 14 to 25, usually 19 to 23, filaments. Gillrakers 8 to 11 + 23 to 26—total 32 to 37, usually 32 to 36. Tubed lateral-line scales 21 to 26, usually 22 to 25. Sum of total number of gillrakers on first arch plus number of tubed lateral-line scales in individual specimens 54 to 60, usually 55 to 60. Circum-caudal-peduncular scales 18 to 21, usually 20. Scales between anal-fin origin and lateral line 11 to 15, usually 12 or 13. Epineurals associated with first 11 to 13 vertebrae. Epurals 3. Lateral aspect of snout usually without scales, lachrymal usually with scales, anterior part of gular region usually with scales. Frequency distributions for countable characters are given in Tables 2–17, and morphometric data for the four species of *Callanthias* (*allporti, legras, parini, ruber*) usually having 10 soft rays in both dorsal and anal fins are presented in Table 18.

Coloration. According to Boulenger (1895:335), this species (as *Callanthias peloritanus*) is "Rose-coloured, sides and fins tinged with yellow." Golani et al. (2006:136) provided an illustration of a specimen that has a pattern of coloration similar to that described by Boulenger. A photograph of *C. ruber* in Brito et al. (2002:236, Foto 227) shows a fish with head reddish above eye, mostly whitish below; body with violet line below dorsal fin and above subdued yellowish band that runs posteriorly to as far as end of base of dorsal fin, remainder of body white except for two broad rosy bars below lateral line—one beneath anterior part of spinous dorsal fin and one beneath most of soft dorsal fin; iris of eye with inner ring of bright yellow and outer ring of dull reddish except bright blue posterodorsally; dorsal, anal, and pelvic fins bright yellow, pectoral fin dull reddish, both lobes of caudal fin and their produced rays bright yellow, middle of caudal fin dull rose. Kuiter (2004:7) has a photograph that shows similar pattern of coloration, except broad swath on head and body from orbit to end of dorsal-fin base bright yellow, venter of body dull yellow to dull orange from pectoral-fin base to posterior end of anal-fin base, some reddish at base and posterior end of anal fin, pectoral fin mostly dull yellow—reddish distally, and pelvic fin reddish distally.

Otoliths. Sanz Echeverría (1931:371; pl. 2, figs. 8 & 9) described and illustrated two of the otoliths (sagitta and lapillus) from *Callanthias ruber* (account labeled as *Callanthias peloritanus*). Nolf (2013:94, pl. 220) provided illustrations of an otolith from a specimen of *C. ruber* collected in the Mediterranean off Nice, France, and of a fossil otolith from Catalonia, Spain (Pliocene, Zanclean Stage), identified as being from *C. ruber.* In addition, Nolf (2013:94, pl. 219) illustrated an otolith from a specimen identified as *Grammatonotus laysanus* obtained from Hawaii and (pl. 220) otoliths from the otlolith-based fossil species "*Callanthiida*" *excavata* (Lower Eocene of southern England) and "? *Callanthiida*" *sulcata* (Upper Eocene of southern England).

Sexuality and dimorphism. Tortonese (1986:782) and Bauchot (1987:1307) stated that this species is probably a protogynous hermaphrodite. The specimens of C. *ruber* that we examined fall into two groups: those with short caudal-fin lobes (n = 3; 81.5–126 mm SL) and those with long caudal-fin lobes (n = 17; 111–177) (Table 20). The differences between the groups may be sex related, but we lack data that would support this interpretation.

Reproduction. In the Mediterranean, *C. ruber* is reproductively active in December and January (Tortonese, 1986:782; Bauchot, 1987:1307).

Early life history. Fage (1918:33–36; figs. 21–23) reported 28 larvae (5–20 mm) of this species (as *Callanthias peloritanus*), described specimens of four sizes (4.5 mm, 6 mm, 8 mm, and 20 mm), and illustrated three individuals. Bertolini (1933:321–323, figs. 253–255) presented descriptions of the early stages (as *C. peloritanus*) as reported by Fage (1918) and added a description and illustration of a 7.5-mm specimen (p. 322, pl. XX, fig. 6). In the preceding year, Sparta (1932) had described the postembryonic development of *C. ruber* (as *C. peloritanus*), based on nine individuals (3.04–7.60 mm), and provided excellent illustrations (figs. 1–9) of those specimens.

Ecological notes. Tortonese (1973:357; 1986:782; Golani et al., 2006:136) noted that *C. ruber* is found in depths of 50 to 500 meters over rocks and mud and in submarine caves. Brito et al. (2002:217) wrote: "Raro. Demersal en los fondos litorales y de la parte superior del talud. Sólo conocemos cinco capturas en el conjunto de las Islas, entre 128 y 300 m de profundidad." (Rare. Demersal in littoral depths and the upper part of the slope. Only known from five captures in all of the [Canary] Islands, between 128 and 300 m depth.)

Distribution. Tortonese (1973:357; 1986:782) gave the distribution of *C. ruber* as eastern Atlantic from the English Channel (occasionally, based on Desbrosses, 1936) to Mauritania, including certain offshore islands—Azores, Madeira, and Canaries—and throughout the Mediterranean and Adriatic. Dooley et al. (1985:17) verified its presence off the Canary Islands (Tenerife), and Arruda (1997:79) and Santos et al. (1997:82) did the same for the Azores. Golani (1996:37) included it in a checklist of eastern Mediterranean marine fishes; Golani et al. (2006:136) presented a short account and illustration of it in their book on eastern Mediterranean fishes; Bilecenoglu et al. (2002:80), in a checklist of the marine fishes of Turkey, remarked upon its occurrence in the Aegean and Mediterranean seas, as did Fricke et al. (2007:80); Uiblein et al. (1999:58, 65, 70; pl. V, fig. 34) reported it from the vicinity of the Great Meteor Seamount; and Harambillet et al. (1976:600) mentioned its occurrence off the Basque coast of France. Maul (1976:41) said that it is found as far south as Angola "where it seems abundant, whereas in Madeira and the Azores it is but rarely taken." We examined specimens collected in the Atlantic off France, Spain/Portugal, Madeira, Morocco, and Meteor Bank and in the Mediterranean off France, Italy, Libya, and Israel in depths of 140 (140–179) to 183 meters.

Miscellaneous. This species is caught by artisanal and sport fishermen and occurs in the bycatch of commercial fishing (Sicily); regularly present in the markets of Morocco, seldom elsewhere (Bauchot, 1987:1307).

Etymology. The specific name *ruber,* Latin for "red," refers to one of the more dominant colors present in this species.

Material examined. Fifty specimens, 74–177 mm SL. **EUROPE,** Bonaparte Collection: USNM 132173 (2 specimens: 92 & 103 mm SL). **FRANCE,** Bay of Biscay: MNHN 37–255 (1: 177). **SPAIN/PORTUGAL:** MNHN 56–23 (6: 105–158). **MADEIRA:** BMNH 1855.11.29.13 (holotype of *Callanthias paradisaeus:* 118), BMNH 99.1.16.1–3 (2: 140 & 142). **MOROCCO:** ZMH 105115 (6: 82–103). **METEOR BANK:** ZMH 107601 (5: 126–160). **MEDITERRANEAN:** ZMUC 6 (1: 139). **FRANCE,** Mediterranean: IRSNB 2003 (1: 140), MNHN 4217 (1: >132). **ITALY,** Bonaparte Collection: ANSP 13624–13636 (13 syntypes of *Anthias buphthalmos:* 74–101). **ITALY** (coast of): RMNH 197 (3: 86–111). **ITALY,** Livorno: USNM 124484 (1: 111). **ITALY,** Sicily: FMNH 63119 (1: 130), MCZ 26401 (1: 153), ZMUC 10 (1: 149), ZMUC 42 (1: 97), ZMUC 119 (1: 119). **LIBYA,** Gulf of Sidra: ZMH 101546 (1: 111). **ISRAEL:** HUJ. F 7254 (1: 77).

OTHER REPORTS OF *CALLANTHIAS*

Gloerfelt-Tarp and Kailola (1984:138–139) presented photographs of two specimens, subsequently lost, that were identified only to *Callanthias*. Those specimens were collected in the eastern Indian Ocean in the southern Indonesian/northwestern Australian region, but no specific locality was given. The specimen in one of those photographs resembles a male of *C. australis* in a photograph in Kuiter (2004:8). Because *C. australis* is known to occur off the western Australian coast to at least as far north as 26°39' S, Gloerfelt-Tarp and Kailola's specimens were most likely *C. australis*.

Kuiter (2004:10) wrote that a population of *Callanthias* observed off northwestern Australia appears to be *C. japonicus*. Because we have not seen any specimens of *Callanthias* from that region and, in view of the close similarity of *C. japonicus* to *C. australis*, and the fact that the known range of *C. australis* is much closer to northwestern Australia than is the range of *C. japonicus*, we think it more likely that the population in question represents *C. australis*.

Chave and Mundy (1994:386, 396) and Chave and Malahoff (1998:101) reported a species of *Callanthias* observed off the Hawaiian Archipelago and Johnston Atoll in 171 to 360 meters over hard substrate with holes and noted that Ralston et al. (1986:147) saw what was apparently the same species at Johnston Atoll in 240 to 330 meters. Chave and Mundy (1994:396) noted that this species is probably new and that "Both sexes yellow and purple in color, small, and had rounded tails. They hovered near holes or among talus near cliffs." Mundy (2005:350) tentatively identified those individuals as representatives of an undescribed species of *Callanthias*. Mundy and Parrish (2004, pl. 1) presented an underwater photograph of a fish tentatively identified as *Grammatonotus macrophthalmus*. That individual, like the ones mentioned above in Chave and Mundy (1994:396), has considerable purple and yellow coloration, but unlike the specimens of Chave and Mundy, the caudal fin is elongated and produced into numerous filaments. The Hawai'i Undersea Research Laboratory (HURL) has photographs of three species of callanthiids. Although individuals in some HURL photographs were formerly identified as belonging to the genus *Callanthias*, they are now considered as *Grammatonotus* (Christopher Kelley, *in litt.* to WDA, 01 May 2013). This is consistent with the way Randall (2007:200) handled the Callanthiidae from the Hawaiian Islands, recognizing only the genus *Grammatonotus*.

We received digital color images of two individuals of *Callanthias* photographed underwater by Avi Klapfer in the Desventuradas Islands off the coast of Chile. On initial examination of the images by the first author, the photographed specimens (Plate 8) were identified as *Callanthias platei*. This identification was largely based on the fact that the only species of *Callanthias* then known from the Desventuradas was *C. platei*. Subsequent examinations of the images by all three authors lead us to question that identification, because the counts of dorsal- and anal-fin rays do not appear to be those usually found in *C. platei*. The photographed specimens may be representatives of *Callanthias parini* or of an undescribed species.

PSEUDOBRANCHIAL FILAMENTS

The pseudobranch is a paired gill-like structure (essentially a hemibranch, i.e., a gill arch with a single row of filaments [Figure 4]) located on the dorsolateral surface of the branchial chamber and apparently serially homologous with "true" gills (Laurent and Dunel-Erb, 1984; Graham, 2006:92). It is found in many, but not all, fishes (some elasmobranchs, *Acipenser, Lepisosteus osseus, Amia calva,* and many teleosts) (Wittenberg and Haedrich, 1974; Laurent and Dunel-Erb, 1984). Pseudobranch morphology is closely correlated "with development of the choroid plexus of the eye of teleosts and *Amia*" (Graham, 2006:92). Functions that have been attributed to the pseudobranch include respiration, osmoregulation, sensory perception (baroreception), and glandular support of retinal function. Also, much attention has been focused on the possibility that the pseudobranch acts as a vascular rete mirabile, functionally associated with vision (Laurent and Dunel-Erb, 1984; Graham, 2006). All of those proposed functions are subject to speculation and controversy. For example, Graham (2006) thought a respiratory function to be unlikely because the afferent blood to the pseudobranch had already been oxygenated in the gills. The vessel carrying blood away from the pseudobranch, the efferent pseudobranchial artery, gives rise to the ophthalmic artery that conveys blood to the eye (Laurent and Dunel-Erb, 1984:287, fig. 1).

Wittenberg and Haedrich (1974:138) suggested "that the pseudobranch acts to modify the incoming arterial blood in such a way that the counter-current multiplication system of the choroid rete may concentrate oxygen without simultaneously building up an untoward concentration of carbon dioxide within the eye." The presence of gill-like lamellae in the pseudobranch and its insertion in the pathway of the blood supply to the choroid rete mirabile of the eye led early on to speculation that the pseudobranch might play a role in vision and more recently has stimulated research into the possibility that it functions in ocular secretion of oxygen (Waser, 2011). If blood were to become supraoxygenated in its passage through the pseudobranch, it might facilitate the functioning of the retina, which has a high metabolic rate. In view of that speculation, one wonders if the number of pseudobranchial filaments might bear some relationship to the oxygen requirements of the retina.

Anderson and Baldwin (2000:375) reported an increase in number of pseudobranchial filaments with increase in standard length in the anthiine serranid *Anthias noeli*. They examined 17 specimens, 62 to 173 mm SL, finding that the number of filaments varied from ca. 22 to 33. In *Callanthias* our findings are similar but with considerable differences in the ranges between highest and lowest numbers of filaments among the species (Table 15). Examination of plotted data (Figures 19–23) shows a distinct positive correlation between increase in number of pseudobranchial filaments and increase in standard length in *Callanthias australis*, *C. japonicus*, and *C. platei*. The relationship between increase in number of filaments and increase in standard length is much weaker in *C. allporti*, *C. legras*, and *C. ruber* and essentially absent in *C. parini*. Interestingly, the species separate into the same two groups with data on pseudobranchial filaments vs. standard length as with counts of soft rays in the dorsal and anal fins. Species usually having 11 soft rays in both dorsal and anal fins show a distinct positive correlation between increase in number of pseudobranchial filaments and increase in standard length, whereas the species usually having 10 soft rays in both fins show a much weaker correlation.

Although counts of pseudobranchial filaments are not useful for the identification of species of *Callanthias*, the increase in number of filaments with growth may be important in the physiology of the species, possibly facilitating the movement from one ecological regime to another. The pseudobranch may be involved in suprasaturating with oxygen the blood bound for the retina. If so, perhaps an increase in surface area resulting from an increase in number of filaments with growth would be advantageous to an individual during its ontogeny. In addition, it is also possible that the adults of the two groups of species exploit habitats that have different light regimes, but we lack data that would allow exploring that possibility.

MODIFIED MIDLATERAL BODY SCALES

Species of *Callanthias* and *Grammatonotus* have a uniquely ornamented series of scales along the body midlaterally (see scanning electron photomicrographs in Figure 2). The surface ornamentation, located in the posterior field of a scale, usually varies from numerous pits, craters, grooves, and low ridges in *Callanthias* to a trench, trench plus a deep groove, trench plus a few pits, or a single pit in *Grammatonotus.* In some scales of *Callanthias* the grooves resemble teardrops, with the bulbous ends of the "drops" positioned anteriorly. Differences in scale ornamentation readily distinguish *Callanthias* from *Grammatonotus.*

The modified scales of *Callanthias* bear a well-developed network of subsurface canals (not visible in scanning electron micrographs) that open into the surface features (ornamentation). The medial side of a scale is characterized by convex areas that correspond to depressions on the lateral surface. Ornamentation is mostly confined to the center of the posterior field of a scale in small fishes (ca. 100 mm SL) and expands as the fish grows so that in larger specimens (ca. 200 mm SL) it covers almost the width of a scale. The ornamentation is usually shaped like a "V" or a flattened "V," but it is sometimes quite dendritic, especially in regenerated scales. We found no describable differences in ornamentation in modified scales among species of *Callanthias.*

Gill and Mooi (1993:329) hypothesized

> that the dorsally positioned lateral line and the peculiar midlateral scales are derived from a disjunct lateral-line condition. . . . in its relatively dorsal position, the lateral line of callanthiids resembles the anterodorsal lateral line of taxa with disjunct lateral lines (e.g., primitive pseudochromids, plesiopids and *Gramma*). . . . the pitted and/or grooved scales of callanthiids occupy a similar position to the posterior lateral line of other taxa with disjunct lateral lines, and the pits and grooves are associated with free neuromasts; this is evidence that the pitted/groove scales are modified lateral-line scales.

Comparative investigations of modified midlateral scales of callanthiids with the lateral-line scales of callanthiids and with those of fishes with disjunct lateral lines are needed in order to comment further on this putative homology.

GEOGRAPHIC DISTRIBUTION

Species of *Callanthias* are widely distributed in temperate and subtropical latitudes off continental and insular coasts. The genus is antiequatorial and nearly antitropical, there being only a relatively small number of records from the tropics, most of those being for *Callanthias parini*. It is notably absent from the North American, Caribbean, Cocos, South American, and Antarctic plates and has only minimal presence on the Pacific and Philippine plates. Its major foci of distribution are on the Eurasian, African, Indo-Australian, and Nazca plates (see Map 5). With regard to the Pacific Plate, its distribution is similar to that of many other taxa that are absent, or nearly so, from the plate, e.g., Batrachoididae, Opistognathidae, Pomatomidae, Pristidae, Rachycentridae, Sciaenidae, Sillaginidae (Springer, 1982). *Callanthias* species have been collected or observed in a broad range of depths (0 [0/15]–659 meters).

DISCUSSION

Three of the species assigned to *Callanthias* (*australis, japonicus,* and *platei*) are very similar morphologically, as can be seen in the morphometric and meristic data presented herein (Figures 6–17, 19–21; Tables 1–17, 19). They are so similar that one could argue that they don't warrant being distinguished at the species level. In fact, Ogilby (1899:173) was of that opinion with regard to *C. australis,* because in his original description of that species he considered it to be a subspecies of *C. platei.*

Gill and Kemp (2002) explored the problem of the taxonomy of widespread Indo-Pacific shore fishes, asserting "that well-diagnosed geographic forms and subspecies should be awarded full-species status" (p. 165). We agree with them and believe that it is even more widely applicable, being relevant to many groups of fishes, such as the Callanthiidae, that are widely distributed in marine waters. A number of studies support Gill and Kemp's thesis. Muss et al. (2001), using data derived from an analysis of the mitochondrial DNA cytochrome b gene, found that populations of the blenniid genus *Ophioblennius* from the western, central, and eastern Atlantic, which Springer (1962), based on morphology, recognized as a single species, appear to represent several species, which they did not describe. (The third author, CCB, has been able to distinguish those species morphologically, based on many more specimens than were available to Springer.) Also, Moura and Castro (2002) showed that populations of the tetraodontid genus *Canthigaster* from the western, central, and eastern Atlantic, which had been usually considered as a single species, actually make up a complex of at least six species. In addition, Anderson and Springer (2005), based on meristic and morphometric data, described two new species of *Symphysanodon* that had been considered previously as populations of two wide-ranging species. One of the new symphysanodontids, a species from the northern Indian Ocean, had been regarded as conspecific with a widespread Atlantic species; the other, a species from the eastern South Pacific, as being conspecific with a very widely distributed Indo-Pacific species.

Based on study of the mitochondrial DNA cytochrome b gene, Bowen et al. (2001) estimated the divergence of the eastern Atlantic trumpetfish *Aulostomus strigosus* from the Indian-Pacific species *A. chinensis* at about 2.5 million years ago, a date agreeing well with the apparent time of establishment of persistent upwelling of cold water off the southern end of Africa in the late Pliocene (Shannon, 1985:109) and the intensification of Northern Hemisphere glaciation in the late Pliocene (2.8–2.3 million years ago; Dwyer et al. 1995; Williams et al. 1997). The present distribution of those two trumpetfishes could have resulted from a rare dispersal event or could be the product of vicariance, namely, the break in the warm water connection between the Indian and South Atlantic oceans (Bowen et al. 2001). Similarly, dispersal, vicariance, or both could have affected the distributions of the species of *Callanthias*.

In view of the preceding comments (modified from Anderson, 2006:414), the facts that the three species of *Callanthias* (*australis*, *japonicus*, and *platei*) of interest here have widely disjunct distributions, that no two of them occur on the same tectonic plate (see Maps 1, 2, 4), and that they display small morphological differences support the recognition of all three as distinct species.

LITERATURE CITED

Ahlstrom, E. H., J. L. Butler, and B. Y. Sumida. 1976. Pelagic stromateoid fishes (Pisces, Perciformes) of the eastern Pacific: Kinds, distributions, and early life histories and observations on five of these from the northwest Atlantic. Bulletin of Marine Science 26(3):285–402.

Aizawa, M., and K. Matsuura. 1990. *Callanthias allporti* Günther, 1876. P. 256, *in:* K. Amaoka, K. Matsuura, T. Inada, M. Takeda, H. Hatanaka, and K. Okada (editors). Fishes collected by the R/V *Shinkai Maru* around New Zealand. Japan Marine Fishery Resource Research Center, Tokyo, pp. 1–411.

Allué, C., D. Lloris, and S. Meseguer. 2000. Colecciones biológicas de referencia (1982–1999) del Instituto de Ciencias del Mar (CSIC): Catálogo de peces. Consejo Superior de Investigaciones Cientificas, Barcelona, pp. 1–198.

Anderson, W. D., Jr. 1999. Callanthiidae. Pp. 2553–2556, *in:* K. E. Carpenter and V. H. Niem (editors). FAO species identification guide for fishery purposes. The living marine resources of the western central Pacific. Vol. 4: Bony fishes part 2 (Mugilidae to Carangidae). Food and Agriculture Organization of the United Nations, Rome. Pp. 2069–2790, color pls. I–VII. [Published in 2000.]

Anderson, W. D., Jr. 2006. *Meganthias carpenteri,* new species of fish from the eastern Atlantic Ocean, with a key to eastern Atlantic Anthiinae (Perciformes: Serranidae). Proceedings of the Biological Society of Washington 119(3):404–417.

Anderson, W. D., Jr. In press. Callanthiidae. Pp. 0000–0000, *in* K. E. Carpenter (editor). The living marine resources of the eastern central Atlantic. Bony fishes. FAO Species Identification Guide for Fishery Purposes. Food and Agriculture Organization of the United Nations, Rome.

Anderson, W. D., Jr., and C. C. Baldwin. 2000. A new species of *Anthias* (Teleostei: Serranidae: Anthiinae) from the Galápagos Islands, with keys to *Anthias* and eastern Pacific Anthiinae. Proceedings of the Biological Society of Washington 113(2):369–385.

Anderson, W. D., Jr., and G. D. Johnson. 1984. A new species of *Callanthias* (Pisces: Perciformes: Percoidei: Callanthiidae). Proceedings of the Biological Society of Washington 97(4):942–950.

Anderson, W. D., Jr., and V. G. Springer. 2005. Review of the perciform fish genus *Symphysanodon* Bleeker (Symphysanodontidae), with descriptions of three new species, *S. mona, S. parini,* and *S. rhax.* Zootaxa, no. 996:1–44.

Arruda, L. M. 1997. Checklist of the marine fishes of the Azores. Arquivos do Museu Bocage, nova série, 3(2):13–164.

Bauchot, M.-L. 1987. Poissons osseux. Pp. 891–1422, *in:* W. Fischer, M.-L. Bauchot, and M. Schneider (editors). Fiches FAO d'identification des espèces pour les besoins de la pêche. (Révision 1). Méditerranée et mer Noire. Zone de pêche 37. Vol. II: Vertébrés. Food and Agriculture Organization of the United Nations (FAO), Rome, pp. i–vi + 761–1529.

Bertolini, F. 1933. Apogonidae, Serranidae. *In:* Uova, larve e stadî giovanili di Teleostei. Fauna Flora Golfo Napoli 38:306–331, figs. 245–256, pls. XV, XIX–XXI.

Bilecenoglu, M., E. Taskavak, S. Mater, and M. Kaya. 2002. Checklist of the marine fishes of Turkey. Zootaxa, no. 113:1–194.

Böhlke, J. E. 1960. Comments on serranoid fishes with disjunct lateral lines, with the description of a new one from the Bahamas. Notulae Naturae (Philadelphia), no. 330:1–11.

Bonaparte, C. L. 1833. Iconografia della fauna italica per le quattro classi degli animali vertebrati. Tomo III: Pesci. Salviucci, Roma.

Boulenger, G. A. 1895. Catalogue of the perciform fishes in the British Museum. 2nd ed. London, pp. i–xx + 1–394, pls. I–XV.

Bowen, B. W., A. L. Bass, L. A. Rocha, W. S. Grant, and D. R. Robertson. 2001. Phylogeography of the trumpetfishes (*Aulostomus*): Ring species complex on a global scale. Evolution 55(5):1029–1039.

Brito, A., P. J. Pascual, J. M. Falcón, A. Sancho, and G. González. 2002. Peces de las Islas Canarias: Catálogo comentado e ilustrado. Francisco Lemus, Arafo, Tenerife, Canary Islands, pp. 1–419, many color photographs.

Chave, E. H., and A. Malahoff. 1998. In deeper waters: Photographic studies of Hawaiian deep-sea habitats and life-forms. University of Hawaii Press, Honolulu.

Chave, E. H., and B. C. Mundy. 1994. Deep-sea benthic fish of the Hawaiian Archipelago, Cross Seamount, and Johnston Atoll. Pacific Science 48:367–409.

Cocco, A. 1829. Su di alcuni nuovi pesci dè mari di Messina. Giornale di Scienze Lettere e Arti per La Sicilia. Anno 7, 26(77):138–147.

Collette, B. B. 2013. Nikolai Vasil'evich Parin (1932–2012), obituary. Copeia 2013(4):768–780.

Desbrosses, P. 1936. Présence à l'entrée occidentale de la Manche de la *Callanthias ruber* (Rafinesque 1810) poisson des eaux Ibérico-Madériennes et Méditerranéennes. Bulletin de la Société Zoologique de France 61:215–219, 406–407.

Doak, W. 1972. Fishes of the New Zealand Region. Hodder and Stoughton, Auckland, Sydney, and London, pp. i–x [unpaginated] + 1–132, 48 color pls., line drawings.

Dooley, J. K., J. van Tassell, and A. Brito. 1985. An annotated checklist of the shorefishes of the Canary Islands. American Museum Novitates, no. 2824:1–49, figs. 1–5.

Dwyer, G. S., T. M. Cronin, P. A. Baker, M. E. Raymo, J. S. Buzas, and T. Corrège. 1995. North Atlantic deepwater temperature change during late Pliocene and late Quaternary climatic cycles. Science 270:1347–1351.

Dyer, B. S., and M. W. Westneat. 2010. Taxonomy and biogeography of the coastal fishes of Juan Fernández Archipelago and Desventuradas Islands, Chile. Revista de Biología Marina y Oceanografiá 45(S1):589–617.

Edgar, G. J., P. R. Last, and M. W. Wells. 1982. Coastal fishes of Tasmania and Bass Strait. Cat & Fiddle Press, Hobart, Tasmania, pp. i–iii [unpaginated] + 6–176; 142 color photos.

Eschmeyer, W. N. (editor). Genera, species, references. Electronic version (http://research.calacademy.org/research/ichthyology/catalog/fishcatmain.asp). Most recently accessed 14 April 2015.

Fage, L. 1918. Shore-fishes. Report on the Danish Oceanographical Expeditions 1908–1910 to the Mediterranaean and adjacent seas. Vol. II: Biology (A. 3), 154 pp., 114 figs., 16 charts.

Fourmanoir, P. 1981. Résultats des Campagnes Musorstom. 1. Philippines (18–28 mars 1976). Poissons (première liste). Mémoires de l'ORSTOM (Office de la Recherche Scientifique et Technique Outre-Mer), no. 91:85–102. [English abstract.]

Fowler, H. W. 1907. Notes on Serranidae. Proceedings of the Academy of Natural Sciences of Philadelphia 59:249–269.

Francis, M. 2012. Coastal fishes of New Zealand. Craig Potton Publishing, Nelson, New Zealand, pp. 1–267, many color figs.

Franz, V. 1910. Die japanischen Knochenfische der Sammlungen Haberer und Doflein. Beiträge zur Naturgeschichte Ostasiens. Abhandlungen der math.-phys. Klasse der K. Bayer. Akademie der Wissenschaften, IV. Suppl.-Bd. 1:1–135, 11 pls., 7 text figs.

Fricke, R., M. Bilecenoglu, and H. Musa Sari. 2007. Annotated checklist of fish and lamprey species (Gnathostomata and Petromyzontomorphi) of Turkey, including a Red List of threatened and declining species. Stuttgarter Beiträge zur Naturkunde, serie A (Biologie), no. 706:1–169.

Gilbert, C. H. 1905. The deep-sea fishes of the Hawaiian Islands. Pp. 575–713, pls. 66–101, *in:* D. S. Jordan and B. W. Evermann. The aquatic resources of the Hawaiian Islands. Bulletin of the United States Fish Commission 23 (for 1903), part II, section II.

Gill, A. C., and J. M. Kemp. 2002. Widespread Indo-Pacific shore-fish species: A challenge for taxonomists, biogeographers, ecologists, and fishery and conservation managers. Environmental Biology of Fishes 65:165–174.

Gill, A. C., and R. D. Mooi. 1993. Monophyly of the Grammatidae and of the Notograptidae, with evidence for their phylogenetic positions among perciforms. Bulletin of Marine Science 52(1):327–350.

Gloerfelt-Tarp, T., and P. J. Kailola. [1984.] Trawled fishes of southern Indonesia and northwestern Australia. The Australian Development Assistance Bureau; The Directorate General of Fisheries, Indonesia; Deutsche Gesellschaft für Technische Zussamenarbeit, Deutschland; printed in Singapore by Tien Wah Press, pp. i–xvi + 1–406, pls. 1–3, many figs.

Golani, D. 1996. The marine ichthyofauna of the eastern Levant—history, inventory and characterization. Israel Journal of Zoology 42:15–55.

Golani, D., B. Öztürk, and N. Başusta. 2006. The fishes of the eastern Mediterranean. Turkish Marine Research Foundation, Istanbul,

Turkey, pp. i–vii [unpaginated] + 8–259, color illus., black and white figs.

Gosline, W. A. 1966. The limits of the fish family Serranidae, with notes on other lower percoids. Proceedings of the California Academy of Sciences, 4th series, 33(6):91–112.

Graham, D. H. 1940. A second specimen of *Calanthias* in New Zealand waters. Transactions of the Royal Society of New Zealand 69:425–426, pl. 58.

Graham, J. B. 2006. Aquatic and aerial respiration. Pp. 85–117, *in:* D. H. Evans and J. B. Claiborne (editors). The physiology of fishes. 3rd ed. CRC Press, Taylor and Francis Group, Boca Raton, Florida.

Gray, C. A., and A. G. Miskiewicz. 2000. Larval fish assemblages in south-east Australian coastal waters: Seasonal and spatial structure. Estuarine, Coastal and Shelf Science 50:549–570.

Griffin, L. T. 1921. Descriptions (with illustrations) of four fishes new to New Zealand. Transactions and Proceedings of the New Zealand Institute 53:351–357, pls. 54 & 55.

Günther, A. 1876. Remarks on fishes, with descriptions of new species in the British Museum, chiefly from southern seas. Annals and Magazine of Natural History, series 4, 17(101):389–402.

Harambillet, G., A. Percier, and J.-C. Quero. 1976. Remarques sur la faune ichtyologique de la côte Basque française. Revue des Travaux de l'Institut des Pêches Maritimes 40(3–4):600.

Heemstra, P. C., and W. D. Anderson Jr. 1986. Family no. 168: Callanthiidae. Pp. 538–539, *in:* M. M. Smith and P. C. Heemstra. Smiths' Sea Fishes. Macmillan South Africa, Johannesburg.

Hubbs, C. L., and K. F. Lagler. 1958. Fishes of the Great Lakes region. Cranbrook Institute of Science, Bulletin 26, Bloomfield Hills, Michigan.

Johnson, G. D. 1975. The procurrent spur: An undescribed perciform caudal character and its phylogenetic implications. Occasional Papers of the California Academy of Sciences 121:1–23.

Johnson, G. D. 1984. Percoidei: Development and relationships. Pp. 464–498, *in:* H. G. Moser et al. (editors). Ontogeny and systematics of fishes. Special Publication No. 1, American Society of Ichthyologists and Herpetologists, Lawrence, Kansas.

Jordan, D. S., and B. W. Evermann. 1896. The fishes of North and Middle America: A descriptive catalogue of the species of fish-like vertebrates found in the waters of North America, north of the Isthmus of Panama, Part I. Bulletin of the United States National Museum, no. 47: pp. i–lx + 1–1240.

Katayama, M. 1959. Studies on the serranid fishes of Japan (I). Bulletin of the Faculty of Education, Yamaguchi University, 8 (Part 2):103–180.

Katayama, M. 1960a. Fauna Japonica Serranidae (Pisces). Biogeographical Society of Japan, Tokyo, pp. i–viii + 1–189, pls. 1–86.

Katayama, M. 1960b. Studies on the serranid fishes of Japan (II). Bulletin of the Faculty of Education, Yamaguchi University, 9 (Part 2):63–98.

Katayama, M. 1984. *Callanthias japonicus*. P. 138, pl. 124-E, *in:* H. Masuda et al. (editors). The fishes of the Japanese Archipelago. Tokai University Press, Tokyo, 2 vols.: text, pp. i–xxii + 1–438; pls. 1–370.

Katayama, M., E. Yamamoto, and T. Yamakawa. 1982. A review of the serranid fish genus *Grammatonotus*, with description of a new species. Japanese Journal of Ichthyology 28(4):368–374.

Kotthaus, A. 1976. Fische des Indischen Ozeans. Ergebnisse der ichthyologischen Untersuchungen während der Expedition des Forschungsschiffes "Meteor" in den Indischen Ozean, Oktober 1964 bis Mai 1965. A. Systematischer Teil, XVII. Percomorphi (7). "Meteor" Forschungsergebnisse. Reihe D, no. 23:45–61.

Kuiter, R. H. 2004. Basslets, hamlets, and their relatives: A comprehensive guide to selected Serranidae and Plesiopidae. The Marine Fish Families Series. TMC Publishing, Chorleywood, United Kingdom, pp. 1–216, many color figs.

Laurent, P., and S. Dunel-Erb. 1984. The pseudobranch: Morphology and function. Pp. 285–323, *in:* W. S. Hoar, D. J. Randall, and J. R. Brett (editors). Fish physiology. Vol. X: Gills, Part B: Ion and water transfer. Academic Press (Harcourt Brace Jovanovich), New York.

Lee, S. C. 1989. First record of the callanthiid fish, *Callanthias japonicus* from Taiwan (Perciformes: Callanthiidae). Bulletin of the Institute of Zoology, Academia Sinica 28(2):153–155.

Lindberg, G. U., and Z. V. Krasyukova. 1969. Fishes of the Sea of Japan and the adjacent areas of the Sea of Okhotsk and the Yellow Sea.

Part 3: Teleostomi. XXIX. Perciformes. Percoidei (XC. Serranidae–CXLIV. Champsodontidae), pp. i–v + 1–498. [1971, English translation of original Russian by Israel Program for Scientific Translations Jerusalem.]

Lowe, R. T. 1839. A supplement to a synopsis of the fishes of Madeira. Proceedings of the Zoological Society of London, part 7:76–92.

Lowe, R. T. 1843. A history of the fishes of Madeira, with original figures from nature of all the species, by Hon. C. E. C. Norton and M. Young. London, 1843–1860, pp. 1–196, 27 pls. [Pt. 1, July 1843:i–xvi + 1–20, pls. I–IV; pt. 2, September 1843:21–52, pls. V–VII; pt. 3, November 1843:53–84, pls. IX–XII; pt. 4, January 1844:85–116, pls. XIII–XVII; pt. 5, October 1860:117–196.]

Masuda, H., C. Araga, and T. Yoshino. 1975. Coastal fishes of southern Japan. Tokai University Press, Tokyo, pp. 1–379, 143 color pls.

Maul, G. E. 1976. The fishes taken in bottom trawls by R. V. "Meteor" during the 1967 seamounts cruises in the northeast Atlantic. "Meteor" Forschungsergebnisse, Reihe D, no. 22:1–69.

McCulloch, A. R. 1934. Check list of the fish and fish-like animals of New South Wales. 3rd ed., with supplement by Gilbert P. Whitley. Royal Zoological Society of New South Wales, Sydney.

Meléndez, R., and C. Villalba. 1992. Nuevos registros y antecedents para la ictiofauna del Archipiélago de Juan Fernández, Chile. Estudios Oceanológicos, Facultad de Recursos del Mar, Universidad de Antofagasta 11:3–29.

Miskiewicz, A. G., C. C. Baldwin, J. M. Leis, and D. S. Rennis. 2000. Callanthiidae. Pp. 280–284, *in:* J. M. Leis and B. M. Carson-Ewart (editors). The larvae of Indo-Pacific coastal fishes: An identification guide to marine fish larvae. Brill, Leiden, pp. i–xx + 1–850, many illus.

Moura, R. L., and R. M. C. Castro. 2002. Revision of Atlantic sharpnose pufferfishes (Tetraodontiformes: Tetraodontidae: *Canthigaster*), with description of three new species. Proceedings of the Biological Society of Washington 115(1):32–50.

Mundy, B. C. 2005. Checklist of the fishes of the Hawaiian Archipelago. Bishop Museum Bulletin in Zoology 6:1–704.

Mundy, B. C., and F. A. Parrish. 2004. New records of the fish genus *Grammatonotus* (Teleostei: Perciformes: Percoidei: Callanthiidae) from the central Pacific, including a spectacular species in the northwestern Hawaiian Islands. Pacific Science 58(3):403–417.

Muss, A., D. R. Robertson, C. A. Stepien, P. Wirtz, and B. W. Bowen. 2001. Phylogeography of *Ophioblennius:* the role of ocean currents and geography in reef fish evolution. Evolution 55(3):561–572.

Nakabo, T. (editor). 2002. Fishes of Japan with pictorial keys to the species. English edition. Tokai University Press, Tokyo, Vol. I, pp. i–lxii + 1–866; Vol. II, pp. i–viii + 867–1749.

Nolf, D. 2013. The diversity of fish otoliths, past and present. Royal Belgian Institute of Natural Sciences, Brussels.

Norman, J. R. 1937. Fishes. B. A. N. Z. Antarctic Research Expedition, 1929–1931. Reports—Series B (Zoology and Botany), Vol. I (Part 2):49–88.

Novikov, N. P., L. S. Kodolov, and G. M. Gavrilov. 1981. Preliminary list of fishes of the Emperor underwater ridge. Pp. 32–35, *in:* N. V. Parin (editor). Fishes of the open ocean. P. P. Shirshov Institute of Oceanology, Academy of Sciences of the USSR, Moscow ("1980"), pp. 1–120. [In Russian with English abstract on p. 115.]

Ogilby, J. D. 1899. Contribution to Australian ichthyology. Proceedings of the Linnean Society of New South Wales 24:154–186.

Okiyama, M. (editor). 1988. An atlas of the early stage fishes in Japan. Tokai University Press, Tokyo.

Parin, N. V. 1990. Preliminary review of fish fauna of the Nazca and Sala y Gómez submarine ridges (southern east Pacific Ocean). Pp. 6–36, *in:* N. V. Parin and V. E. Becker (editors). Seamount fishes. Transactions of the P. P. Shirshov Institute of Oceanology, Academy of Sciences of the USSR, Vol. 125, pp. 1–224. [In Russian with English summary on p. 36.]

Parin, N. V. 1991. Fish fauna of the Nazca and Sala y Gomez submarine ridges, the easternmost outpost of the Indo-west Pacific zoogeographic region. Bulletin of Marine Science 49(3):671–683.

Parin, N. V., G. A. Golovan, N. P. Pakhorukov, Yu. I. Sazonov, and Yu. N. Shcherbachev. 1981. Fishes from the Nazca and Sala-y-Gomez underwater ridges collected in cruise of R/V "Ikhtiandr." Pp. 5–18, *in:* N. V. Parin (editor in chief). Fishes of the open ocean. P. P. Shirshov Institute of Oceanology, Academy of Sciences of the USSR, Moscow ("1980"), pp. 1–120. [In Russian with English abstract on p. 115.]

Parin, N. V., A. N. Mironov, and K. N. Nesis. 1997. Biology of the Nazca and Sala y Gómez submarine ridges, an outpost of the Indo-west Pacific fauna in the eastern Pacific Ocean: Composition and distribution of the fauna, its communities and history. *In:* The biogeography of the oceans. Advances in Marine Biology 32:145–242.

Pequeño, G. 1989. Peces de Chile. Lista sistemática revisada y comentada. Revista de Biología Marina, Valparaiso, 24(2):1–132.

Pequeño, G., and J. Lamilla. 2000. The littoral fish assemblage of the Desventuradas Islands (Chile) has zoogeographical affinities with the western Pacific. Research Letter, Global Ecology and Biogeography 9:431–437.

Pequeño, G., and S. Sáez. 2000. Los peces litorales del archipiélago de Juan Fernández (Chile): Endemismo y relaciones ictiogeográficas. Investigaciones Marinas, Valparaiso, 28:27–37.

Rafinesque, C. S. 1810. Caratteri di alcuni nuovi generi e nuove specie di animali e piante della Sicilia, con varie osservazioni sopra i medesimi. Part 1. Sanfilippo, Palermo, pp. [i–iv], 3–69.

Ralston, S., R. M. Gooding, and G. M. Ludwig. 1986. An ecological survey and comparison of bottom fish resource assessments (submersible versus handline fishing) at Johnston Atoll. Fishery Bulletin 84(1):141–155.

Randall, J. E. 2007. Reef and shore fishes of the Hawaiian Islands. Sea Grant College Program, University of Hawai'i, Honolulu, i–xiv + 1–546, many color illus.

Rendahl, H. 1921. The fishes of the Juan Fernandez Islands. Pp. 49–58, *in:* C. Skottsberg (editor). The natural history of Juan Fernandez and Easter Island, Vol. 3 (Part 1). Uppsala: Almquist & Wiksells Boktryckeri.

Rivaton, J. 1989. Premières observations sur la faune ichtyologique des iles Chesterfield (mer du Corail). Cybium 13(2):139–164, pls. 1 & 2.

Roberts, C. D. 1993. Comparative morphology of spined scales and their phylogenetic significance in the Teleostei. Bulletin of Marine Science 52(1):60–113.

Roberts, C. D. 1996. Spendid Perch: Northern and southern beauties. Something fishy from MoNZ. New Zealand Fishing News, November:44.

Roberts, C. D., and M. F. Gomon. 2008. Family Callanthiidae splendid perches. Pp. 548–549, *in:* M. Gomon, D. Bray, and R. Kuiter (editors). Fishes of Australia's southern coast. Reed New Holland, Sydney, pp. 1–928.

Robinson, G. 2008. Plate, Ludwig Hermann. Complete dictionary of scientific biography. Accessed 15 September 2013, from Encyclopedia.com, http://www.encyclopedia.com/doc/1G2-2830903441.html.

Santos, R. S., F. M. Porteiro, and J. P. Barreiros. 1997. Marine fishes of the Azores. Annotated checklist and bibliography. Arquipélago—Life and Marine Sciences, Bulletin of the University of the Azores, Suppl. 1:i–xxviii + 1–244.

Sanz Echeverría, J. 1931. Investigaciones sobre otolitos de peces de España. Boletín de la Sociedad Española de Historia Natural 31:369–374, 1 pl.

Saunders, B. 2012. Discovery of Australia's fishes: A history of Australian ichthyology to 1930. CSIRO Publishing, Collingswood, Victoria, pp. i–xii + 1–491, 16 color pls., many black and white illus.

Schmidt, P. J. 1931. Fishes of Japan, collected in 1901. Transactions of the Pacific Committee of the Academy of Sciences of the U.S.S.R. 2:1–176.

Scott, E. O. G. 1979. Observations on some Tasmanian fishes: Part XXV. Papers and Proceedings of the Royal Society of Tasmania 113:99–148.

Senou, H., K. Matsuura, and G. Shinohara. 2006. Checklist of fishes in the Sagami Sea with zoogeographical comments on shallow water fishes occurring along the coastlines under the influence of the Kuroshio Current. Memoirs of the National Science Museum, Tokyo, no. 41:389–542.

Sepúlveda, J. I. 1987. Peces de las islas oceánicas chilenas. Pp. 225–245, *in:* J. C. Castilla (editor). Islas oceánicas chilenas: Conocimiento cientifico y necesidades de investigaciónes. Ediciones Universidad Católica de Chile, Santiago.

Sepúlveda, J. I., and G. Pequeño. 1985. Fauna íctica del archipiélago de Juan Fernández. Pp. 81–91, *in:* P. Arana (editor). Investigaciones Marinas en el Archipiélago de Juan Fernández.

Shannon, L. V. 1985. The Benguela ecosystem. Part I: Evolution of the Benguela, physical features and processes. Oceanography and Marine Biology: An Annual Review 23:105–182.

Shinohara, G., H. Endo, K. Matsuura, Y. Machida, and H. Honda. 2001. Annotated checklist of the deepwater fishes from Tosa Bay, Japan. National Science Museum Monographs, Tokyo, no. 20:283–343.

Shinohara, G., and K. Matsuura. 1997. Annotated checklist of deep-water fishes from Suruga Bay, Japan. National Science Museum Monographs, no. 12:269–318, pls. 1–2.

Shinohara, G., T. Sato, Y. Aonuma, H. Horikawa, K. Matsuura, T. Nakabo, and K. Sato. 2005. Annotated checklist of deep-sea fishes from the waters around the Ryukyu Islands, Japan. *In:* K. Hasegawa, G. Shinohara, and M. Takeda (editors). Deep-sea fauna and pollutants in the Nansei Islands. National Science Museum Monographs, Tokyo, no. 29:385–452.

Shinohara, G., S. M. Shirai, M. V. Nazarkin, and M. Yabe. 2011. Preliminary list of the deep-sea fishes of the Sea of Japan. Bulletin of the National Museum of Nature and Science, series A, 37(1):35–62.

Smith, J. L. B. 1948. Brief revisions and new records of South African marine fishes. Annals and Magazine of Natural History, series 11, 14(113):335–346.

Smith, J. L. B. 1955. The fishes of the family Anthiidae of the western Indian Ocean. Annals and Magazine of Natural History, series 12, 8(89):337–350.

Smith, J. L. B. 1961. Fishes of the family Anthiidae from the western Indian Ocean and the Red Sea. Ichthyological Bulletin, Department of Ichthyology, Rhodes University, no. 21:359–369, pls. 34 & 35.

Smith, M. M. 1980. Marine fishes of Maputaland. Pp. 164–187, *in:* M. N. Bruton and K. H. Cooper. Studies on the ecology of Maputaland. Rhodes University, Grahamstown, and the Wildlife Society, Durban.

Smith, M. M., and P. C. Heemstra (editors). 1986. Smiths' sea fishes. Macmillan South Africa, Johannesburg, pp. i–xx + 1–1047, 144 color pls., many black and white figs.

Sparta, A. 1932. Contributo alla conoscenza dello sviluppo post-embrionale di *Callanthias peloritanus* Gthr. R. Comitato Talassografica Italiano, Memoria 197, 10 pp., 9 figs.

Springer, V. G. 1962. A review of the blenniid fishes of the genus *Ophioblennius* Gill. Copeia 1962 (2): 426–433.

Springer, V. G. 1982. Pacific plate biogeography, with special reference to shorefishes. Smithsonian Contribution to Zoology, no. 367, pp. i–iv + 182.

Springer, V. G., and G. D. Johnson. 2004. Study of the dorsal gill-arch musculature of teleostome fishes, with special reference to the Actinopterygii. Appendix: V. G. Springer and T. M. Orrell—Phylogenetic analysis of 147 families of acanthomorph fishes based primarily on dorsal gill-arch muscles and skeleton. Bulletin of the Biological Society of Washington no. 11, 2 vols.: text, pp. i–vi + 1–260; pls. 1–205.

Steindachner, F. 1898. Die Fische der Sammlung Plate. *In:* Fauna Chilensis. Abhandlungen zur Kenntniss der Zoologie Chiles nach den Sammlungen von Dr. L. Plate. Erster Band, Zweites Heft, pp. 281–338, pls. 15–21. Zoologische Jahrbücher, Suppl.-Bd. IV, Jena.

Tanaka, S. 1922. Figures and descriptions of the fishes of Japan including Riukiu Islands, Bonin Islands, Formosa, Kurile Islands, Korea, and southern Sakhalin. 32:583–606, pls. 145–147. [In Japanese and English.]

Tortonese, E. 1972. On the affinities and systematic position of the genus *Callanthias* after a study of its type species *C. ruber* (Raf.) (Pisces Percoidei). Bolletino di Zoologia 39(1):71–82.

Tortonese, E. 1973. Serranidae. Pp. 355–362, *in:* J. C. Hureau and Th. Monod (editors). Check-list of the fishes of the north-eastern Atlantic and of the Mediterranean (Clofnam), Vol. I. UNESCO, Paris, pp. i–xxii + 1–683.

Tortonese, E. 1986. Serranidae. Pp. 780–792, *in:* P. J. P. Whitehead, M.-L. Bauchot, J.-C. Hureau, J. Nielsen, and E. Tortonese (editors). Fishes of the North-eastern Atlantic and the Mediterranean, Vol. II. UNESCO. Paris, pp. 517–1007.

Trnski, T., and A. G. Miskiewicz. 1998. Callanthiidae: Yellow-fin basses. Pp. 189–191, *in:* F. J. Neira, A. G. Miskiewicz, and T. Trnski (editors). Larvae of temperate Australian fishes: Laboratory guide for larval fish identification. University of Western Australia Press, Nedlands, Western Australia, pp. i–xx + 1–474, many illus.

Uiblein, F., A. Geldmacher, F. Köster, W. Nellen, and G. Kraus. 1999. Species composition and depth distribution of fish species collected in the area of the Great Meteor Seamount, eastern central Atlantic, during cruise M42/3, with seventeen new records. Informes Técnicos del Instituto Canario de Ciencias Marinas, no. 5:47–79, pls. 1–5.

Waite, E. R. 1899. Scientific results of the trawling expedition of H. M. C. S. "Thetis," off the coast of New South Wales, in February and March, 1898. Australian Museum, Sydney, Memoir 4 (Part 1):2–132, pls. 1–31.

Waser, W. 2011. Root effect: Root effect definition, functional role in oxygen delivery to the eye and swimbladder. Pp. 929–934, *in:* A. Farrell (editor in chief). Encyclopedia of fish physiology: From genome to environment. Elsevier, Amsterdam, 2272 pp.

Williams, D. F., J. Peck, E. B. Karabanov, A. A. Prokopenko, V. Kravchinsky, J. King, and M. I. Kuzmin. 1997. Lake Baikal record of continental climate response to orbital insolation during the past five million years. Science 278:1114–1117.

Wittenberg, J. B., and R. L. Haedrich. 1974. The choroid rete mirabile of the fish eye. II. Distribution and relation to the pseudobranch and to the swimbladder rete mirabile. Biological Bulletin 146:137–156.

Yamakawa, T. 1985. *Callanthias japonicus* Franz. *In:* O. Okamura, Y. Machida, T. Yamakawa, K. Matsuura, and T. Yatou. Fishes of the Okinawa Trough and the adjacent waters. II. The intensive research of unexploited fishery resources on continental slopes. Japan Fisheries Resource Conservation Association, Tokyo, 2:418–781, pls. 206–418. [In Japanese and English.]

PLATES

Plate 1. A. *Callanthias allporti.* Tasmania; lectotype, BMNH 1875.11.12.38, 191 mm SL. Photograph by James Maclaine. **B.** *Callanthias allporti.* New Zealand. Photograph by Malcolm Francis, published in Francis (2012).

Plate 2. A. *Callanthias australis*. North of Port Jackson, New South Wales; lectotype, AMS I.3973, 166 mm SL. Photograph by Sandra Raredon. **B.** *Callanthias splendens* (= *Callanthias australis*). Entrance to Hauraki Gulf, Auckland, New Zealand; holotype, AIM MA773, 183 mm SL. Photograph by Sandra Raredon. **C.** *Callanthias australis*. New Zealand; male above, female below. Photograph by Malcolm Francis, published in Francis (2012). **D.** *Callanthias australis*. New Zealand; spawning male. Photograph by Warren Farrelly, published in Francis (2012).

Plate 3. A. *Callanthias japonicus.* Off southwestern Taiwan; ASIZP 0056326, 233 mm SL. Photograph by Sandra Raredon. **B.** *Callanthias japonicus.* Tokai Aquarium, Japan. Photograph by Rudie H. Kuiter, published in Kuiter (2004).

Plate 4. A. *Callanthias legras.* Off Algoa Bay, South Africa; holotype, SAIAB 30, 169 mm SL. Painting by Margaret M. Smith, published in Smith and Heemstra (1986). © South African Institute for Aquatic Biodiversity. Photograph courtesy of South African Institute for Aquatic Biodiversity. **B.** *Callanthias legras.* Agulhas Bank, South Africa; SAIAB 38422, ca. 25 cm TL. Photograph by Phillip C. Heemstra.

Plate 5. A. *Callanthias parini.* Nazca Ridge, eastern South Pacific; holotype, USNM 265444, 175 mm SL. Photograph by James F. McKinney, published in Anderson and Johnson (1984). **B.** *Callanthias parini.* Nazca Ridge, eastern South Pacific. Photograph received from N. V. Parin.

Plate 6. A. *Callanthias platei.* Juan Fernández Islands, eastern South Pacific; lectotype, ZMB 15624, 172 mm SL. Photograph by Sandra Raredon. **B.** *Callanthias platei.* Robinson Crusoe Island, Juan Fernández Islands, eastern South Pacific. Photograph by Pedro Niada, published in Kuiter (2004).

Plate 7. A. *Callanthias paradisaeus* (= *Callanthias ruber*). Madeira; holotype, BMNH 1855.11.29.13, 118 mm SL. Photograph by James Maclaine. **B.** *Callanthias ruber.* Coast of Italy. Photograph by Francesco Costa, published in Kuiter (2004).

Plate 8. *Callanthias* sp. Desventuradas Islands (off the coast of Chile). Photograph by Avi Klapfer, permission for use received from Avi Klapfer and Enric Sala.

FIGURES

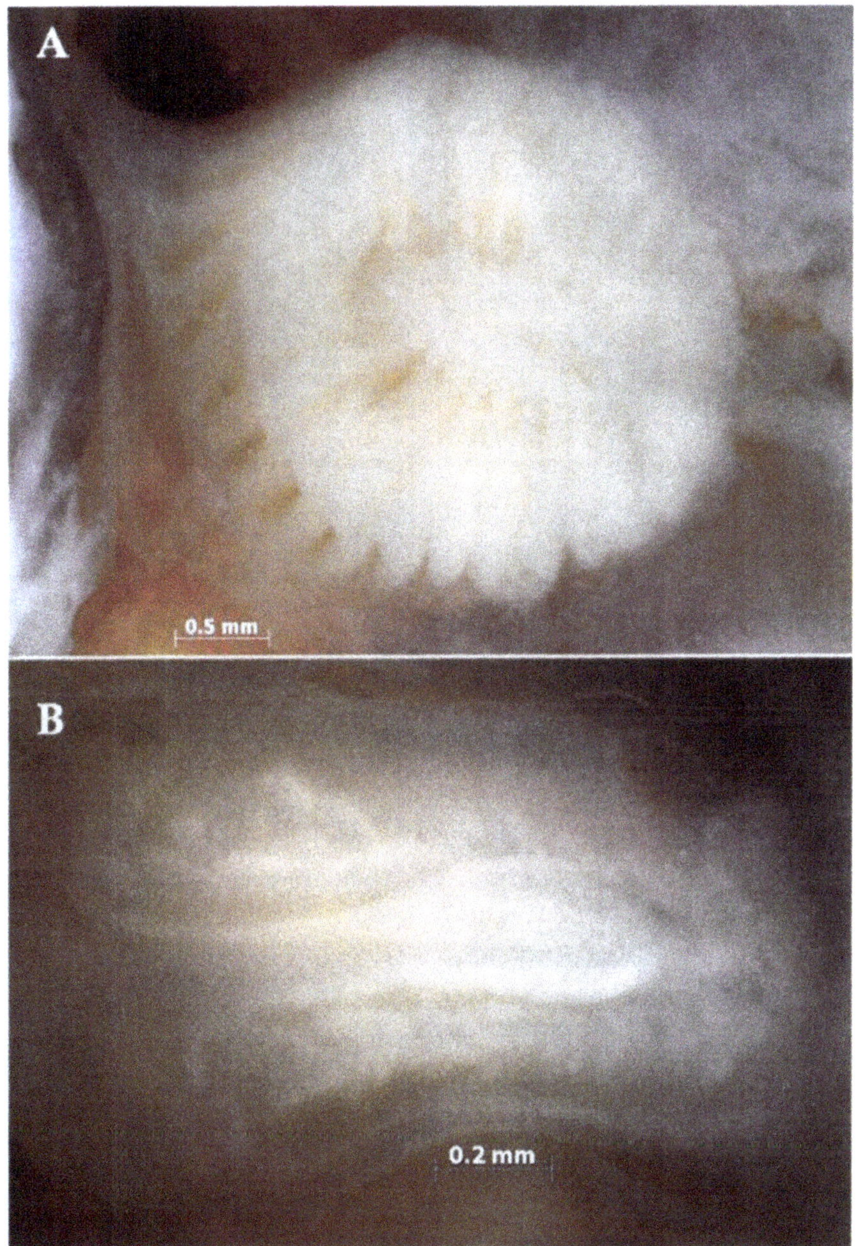

Figure 1. Nasal lamellae. **A.** Well developed in *Micropterus salmoides:* USNM 366392, 86.8 mm SL. **B.** Poorly developed in *Callanthias australis:* AMS I. 31186001, 44 mm SL.

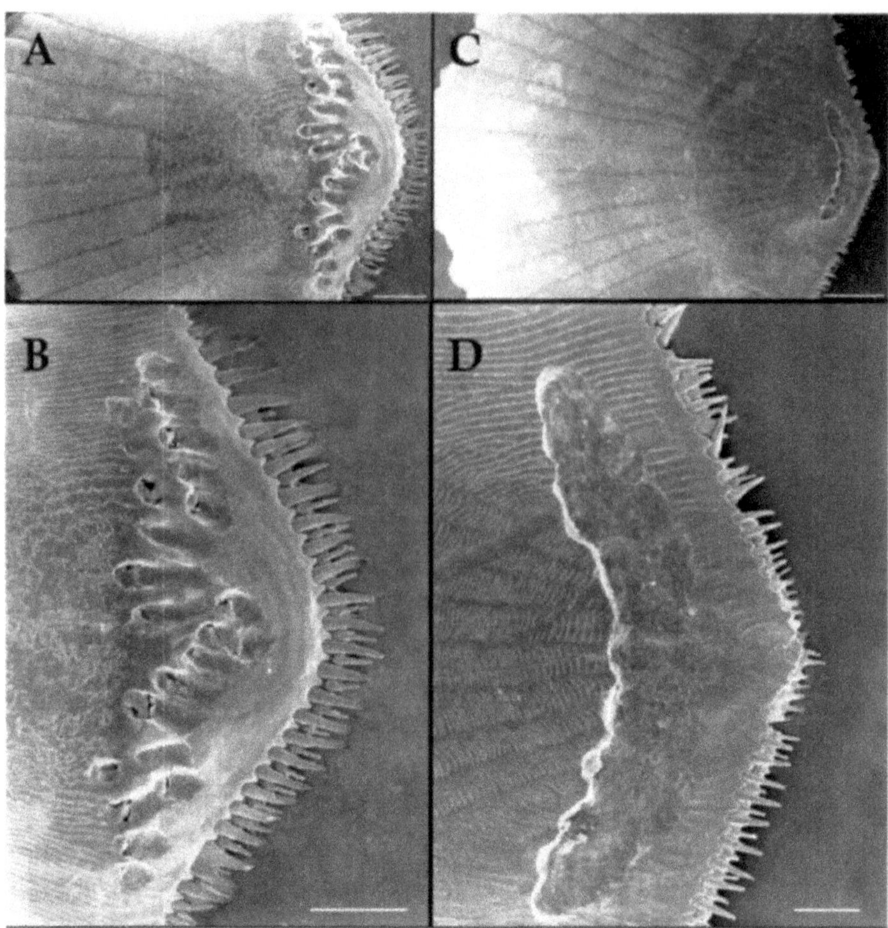

Figure 2. Modified midlateral body scales. Scanning electron photomicrographs, lateral views: **A** & **B.** *Callanthias australis:* LACM 42624–5, 113 mm SL; scale bars in **A** & **B**, each = 500 µm. **C.** & **D.** *Grammatonotus crosnieri:* MUSORSTOM 2, station 12, 117 mm SL; scale bar in **C** = 100 µm, in **D** = 200 µm.

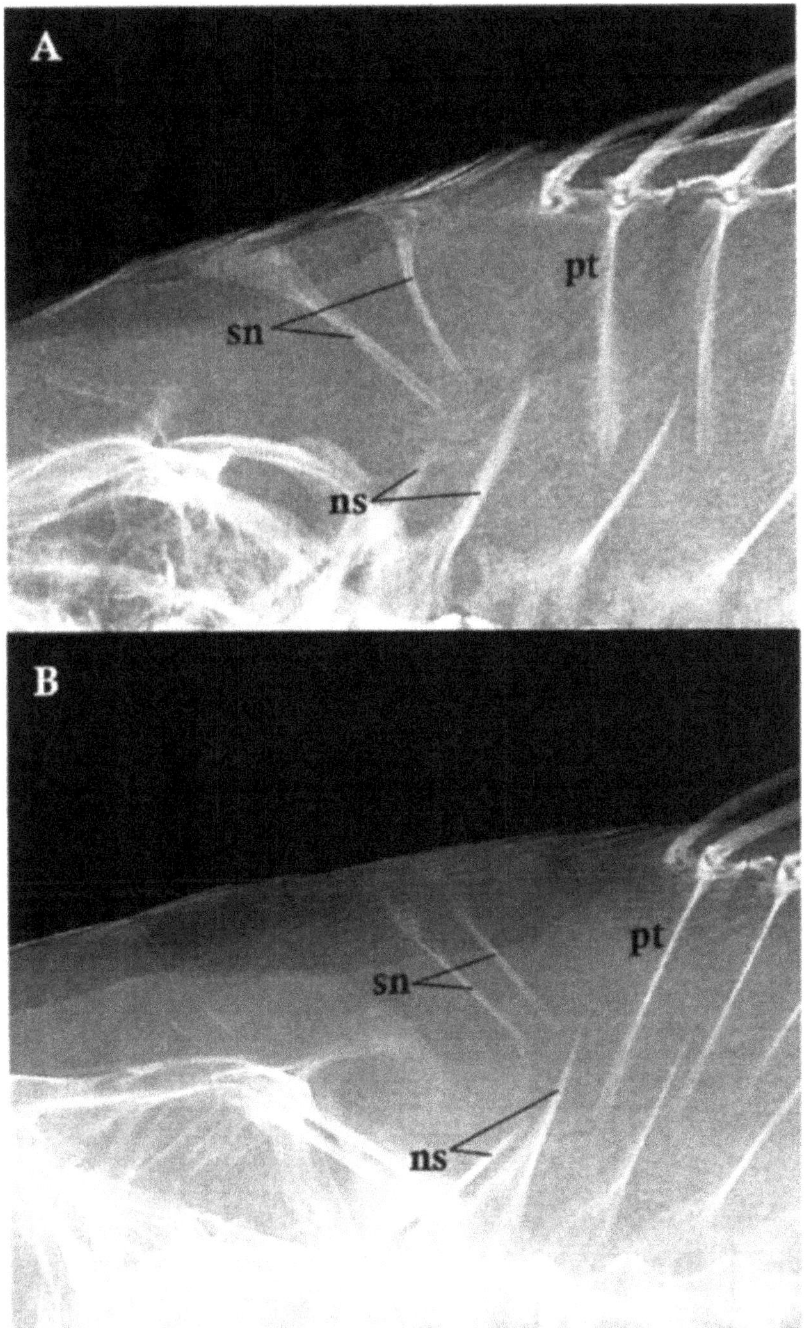

Figure 3. Configurations of supraneural bones, anterior neural spines, and anterior dorsal pterygiophores in callanthiid fishes; **ns** = neural spine, **pt** = dorsal pterygiophore, **sn** = supraneural bone. **A.** *Callanthias japonicus*, ZUMT 51007, 138 mm SL. **B.** *Grammatonotus laysanus*, USNM 150525, 59 mm SL.

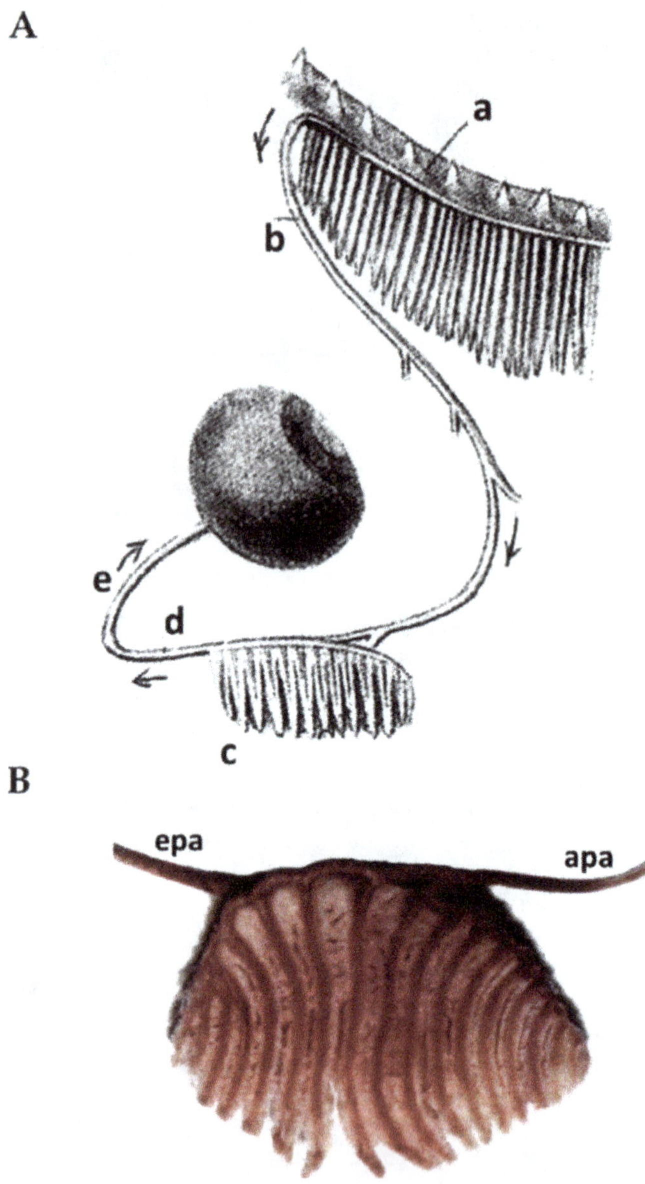

Figure 4. Pseudobranch. **A.** Vascular connections—first gill arch → pseudobranch → eye: **a** = first gill arch, **b** = afferent pseudobranchial artery carrying oxygenated blood, **c** = pseudobranch, **d** = efferent pseudobranchial artery, **e** = ophthalmic artery. **B.** Vasculature of pseudobranch in Rainbow Trout—arteries in gill filaments dark red, gill lamellae light red: **apa** = afferent pseudobranchial artery, **epa** = efferent pseudobranchial artery. Modified after Waser (2011, figs. 4 & 5), used by permission of Elsevier Books, Amsterdam.

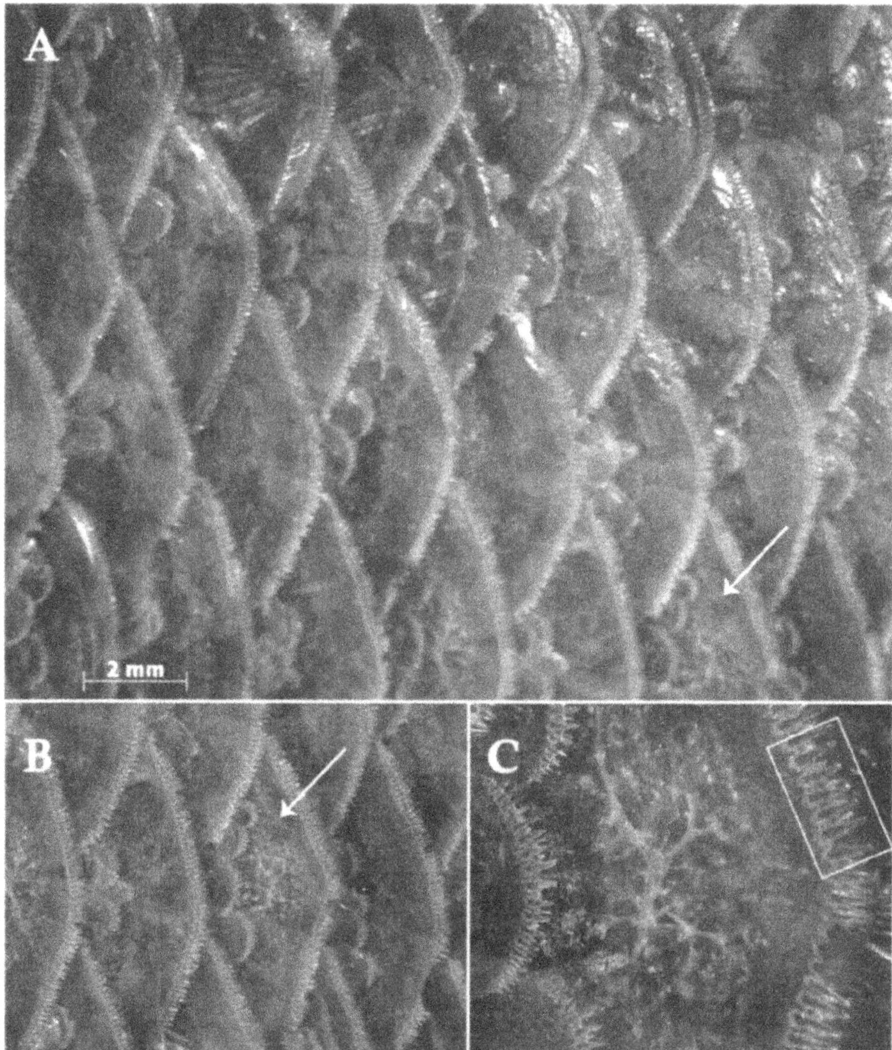

Figure 5. Ctenoid scales with only marginal cteni (i.e., no ctenial bases in the posterior field) as seen in *Callanthias japonicus* (ZUMT 51007, 138 mm SL). Secondary squamation and superficial "canal" system constituting the ornamentation on modified midlateral body scales apparent in **A**, **B**, & **C**. Primary and secondary scalelets (marginal cteni) outlined by rectangle in **C**.

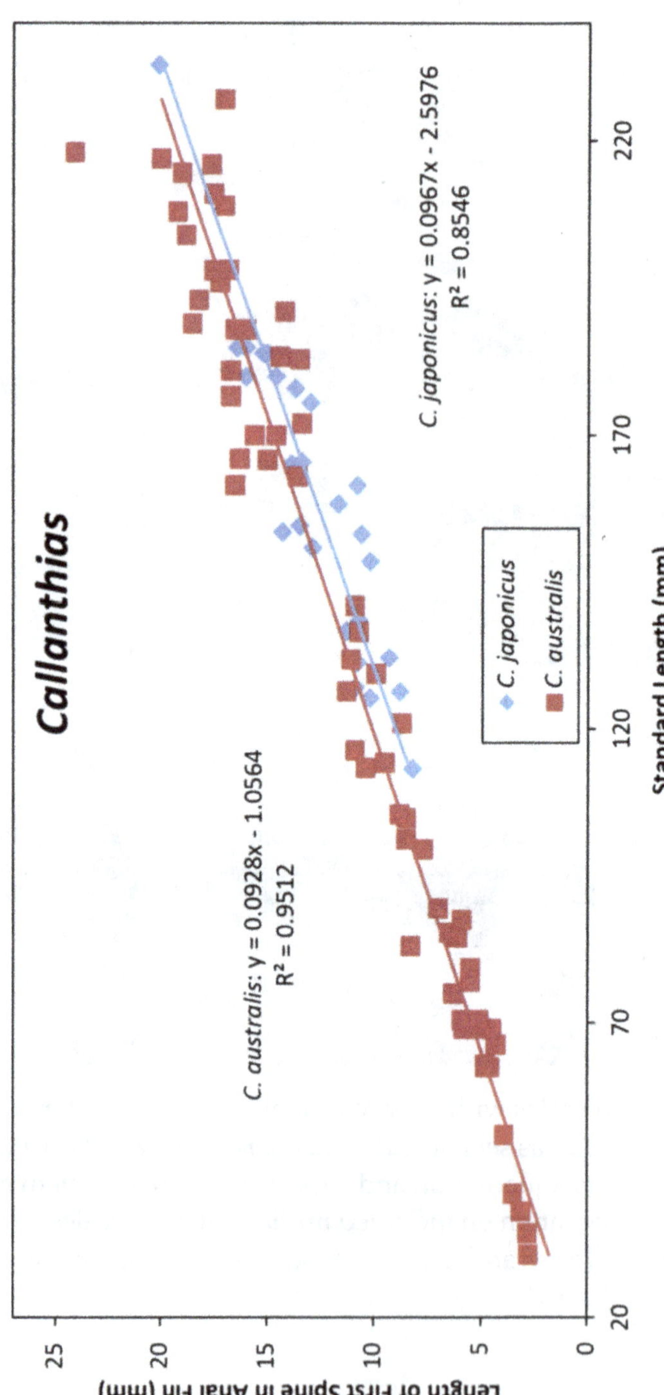

Figure 6. Comparison of length of first spine in anal fin versus standard length in *Callanthias australis* and *C. japonicus.*

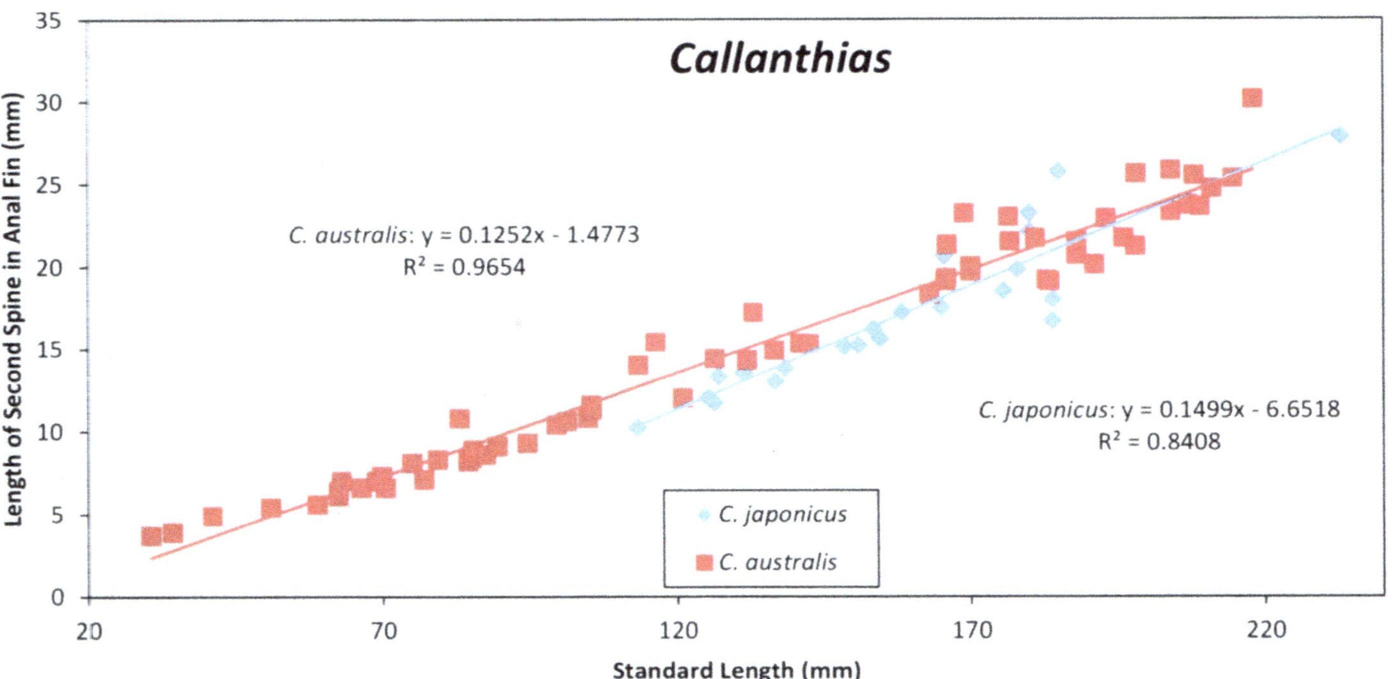

Figure 7. Comparison of length of second spine in anal fin versus standard length in *Callanthias australis* and *C. japonicus*.

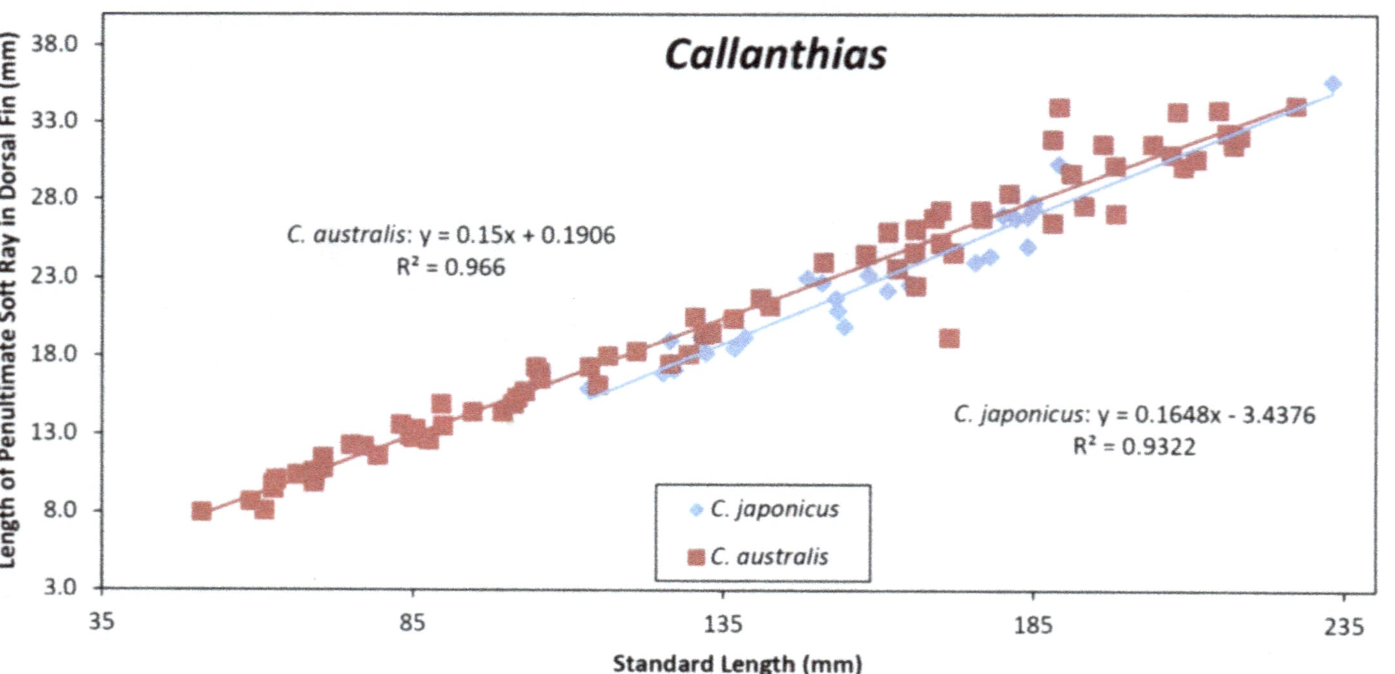

Figure 8. Comparison of length of penultimate soft ray in dorsal fin versus standard length in *Callanthias australis* and *C. japonicus.*

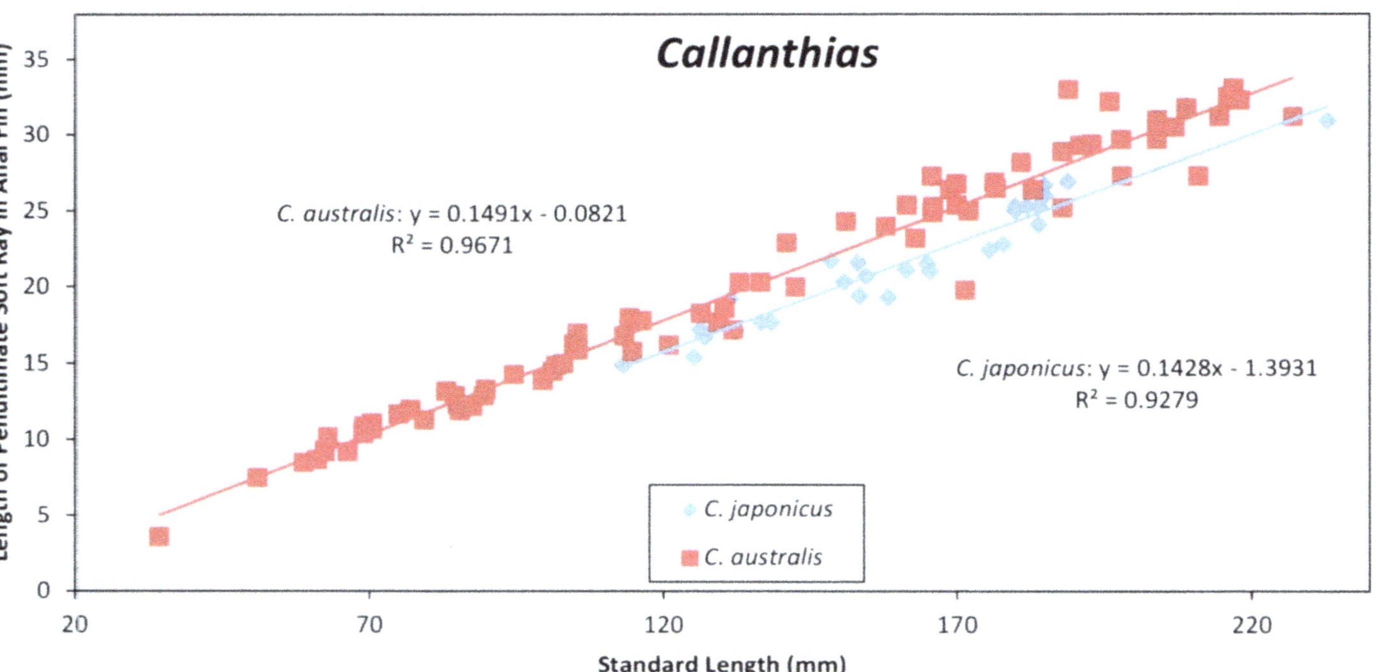

Figure 9. Comparison of length of penultimate soft ray in anal fin versus standard length in *Callanthias australis* and *C. japonicus.*

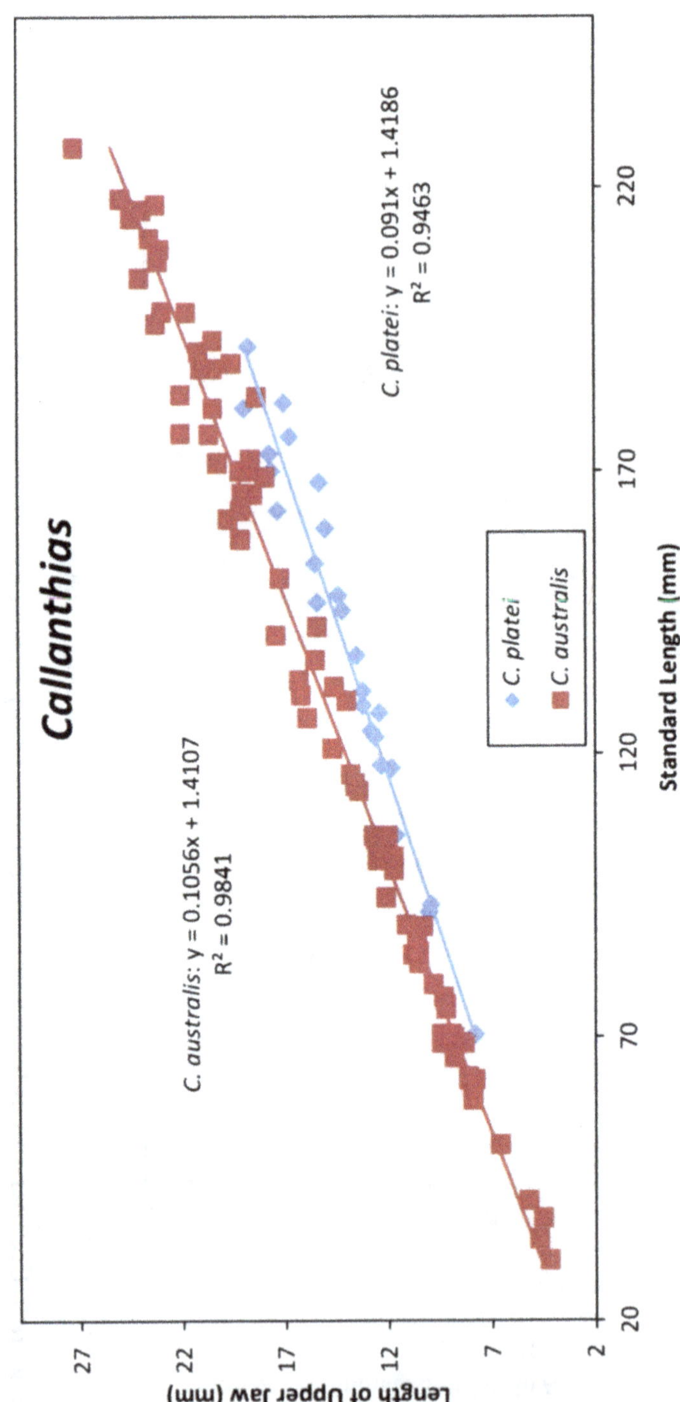

Figure 10. Comparison of length of upper jaw versus standard length in *Callanthias australis* and *C. platei.*

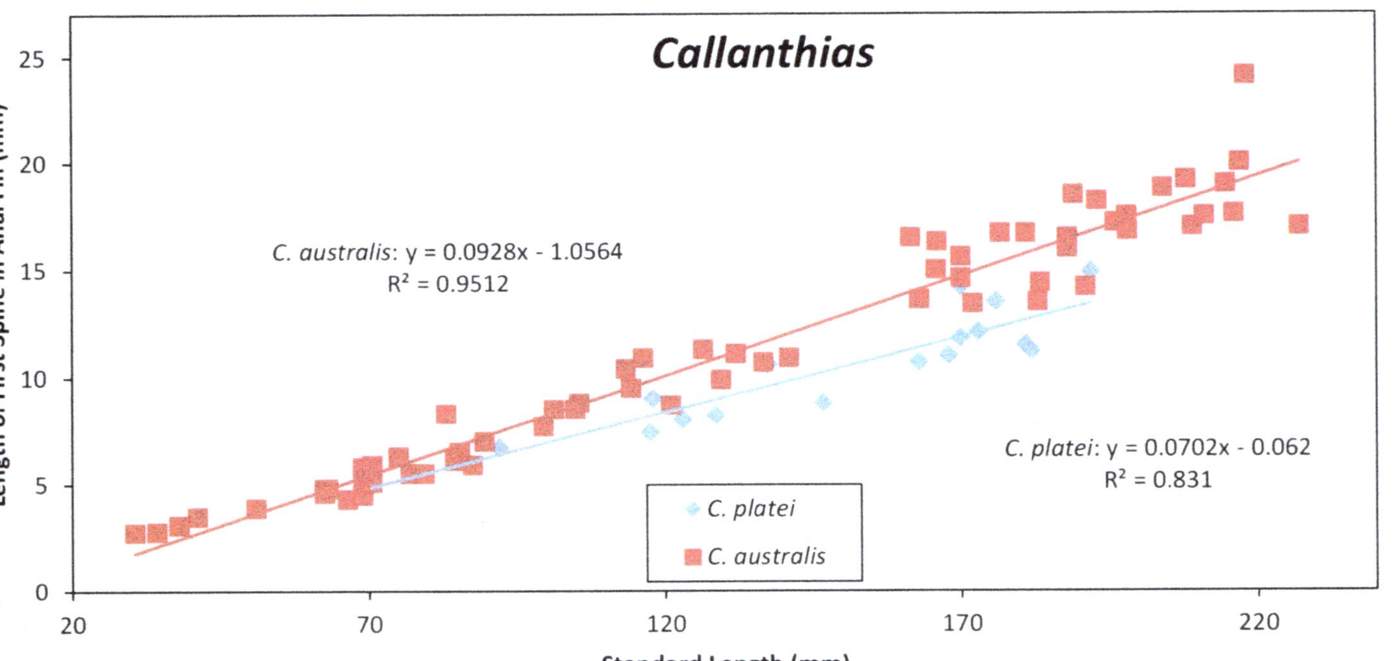

Figure 11. Comparison of length of first spine in anal fin versus standard length in *Callanthias australis* and *C. platei.*

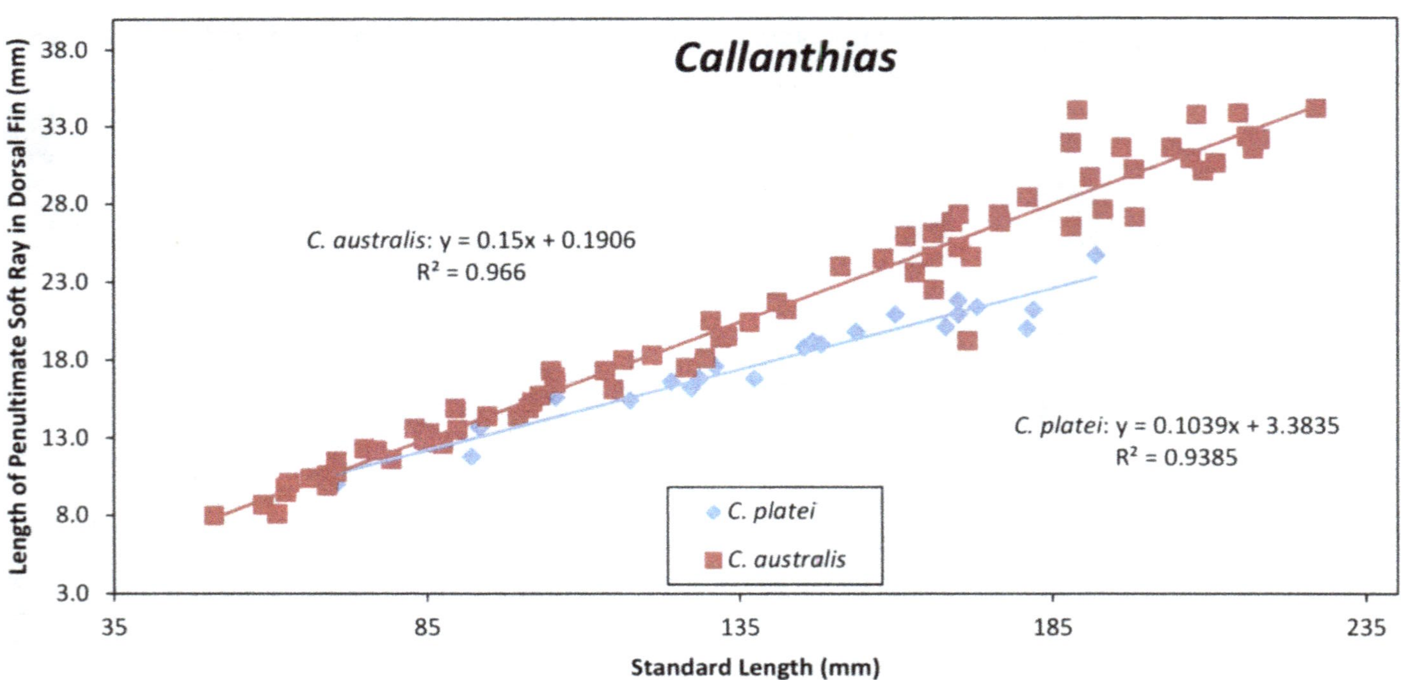

Figure 12. Comparison of length of penultimate soft ray in dorsal fin versus standard length in *Callanthias australis* and *C. platei*.

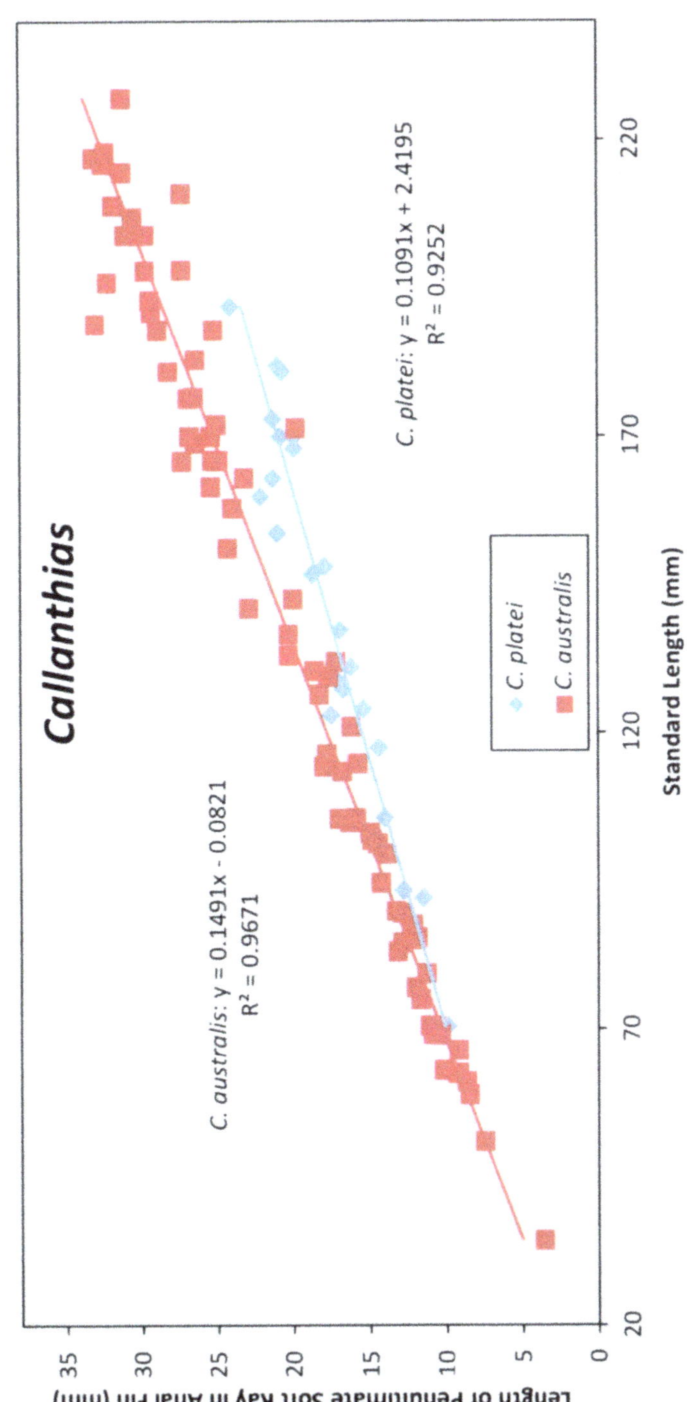

Figure 13. Comparison of length of penultimate soft ray in anal fin versus standard length in *Callanthias australis* and *C. platei.*

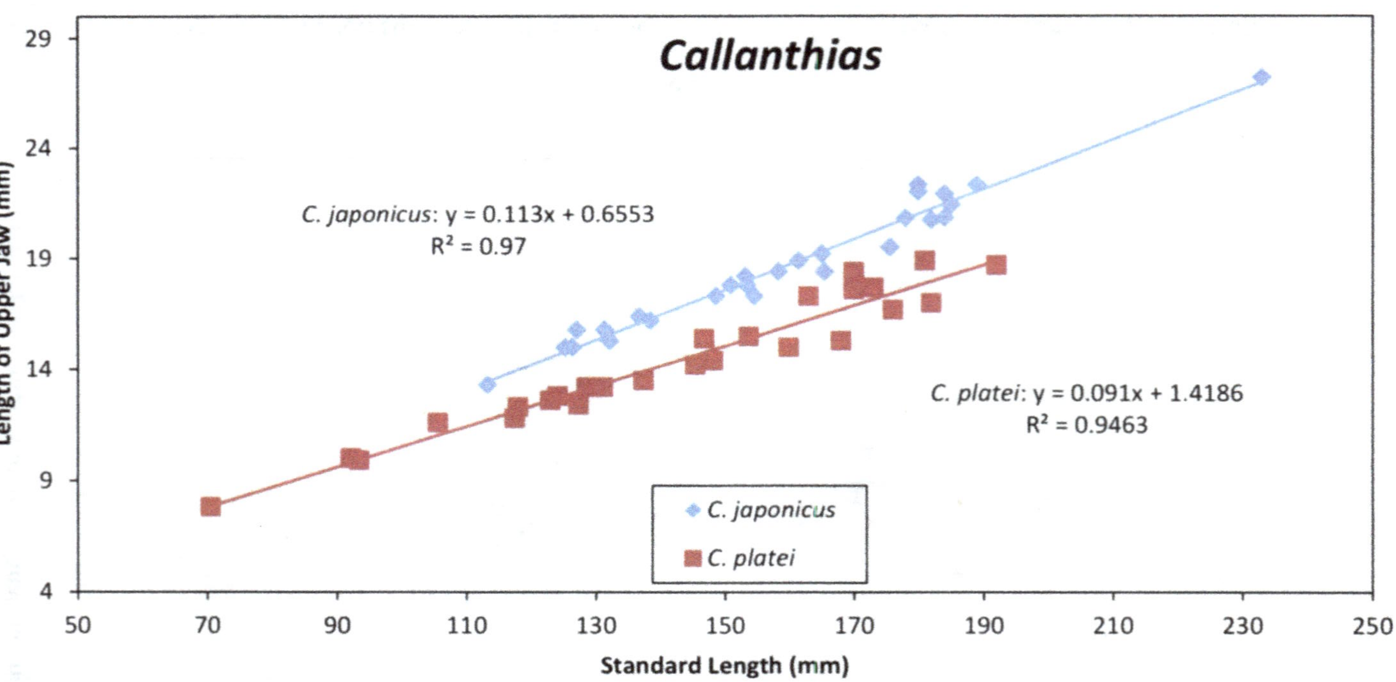

Figure 14. Comparison of length of upper jaw versus standard length in *Callanthias japonicus* and *C. platei.*

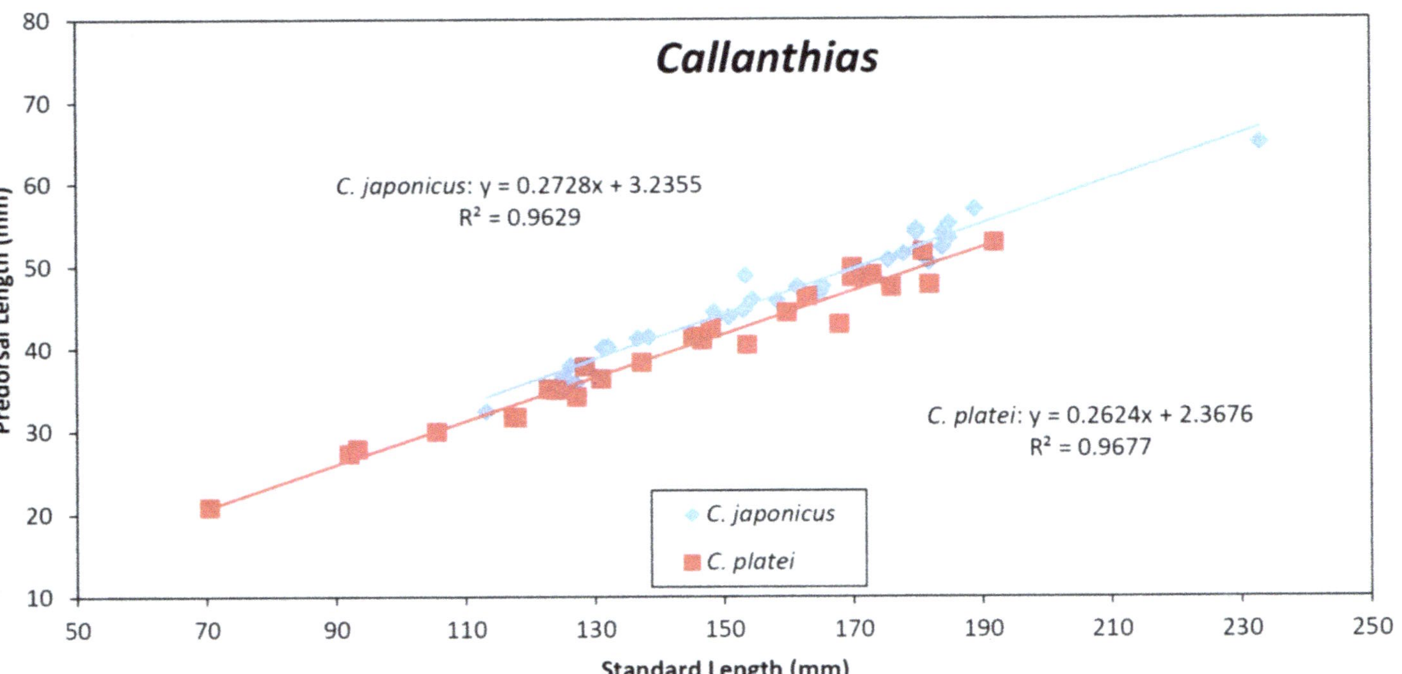

Figure 15. Comparison of predorsal length versus standard length in *Callanthias japonicus* and *C. platei.*

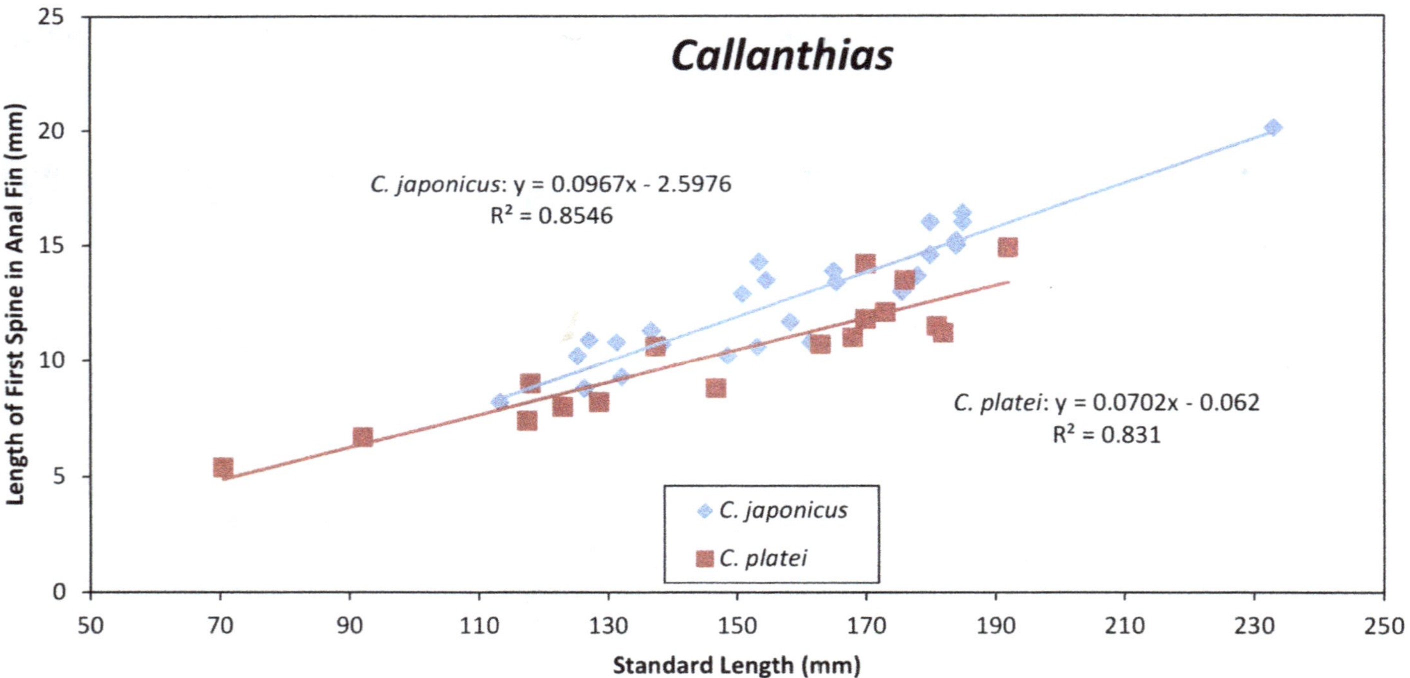

Figure 16. Comparison of length of first spine in anal fin versus standard length in *Callanthias japonicus* and *C. platei*.

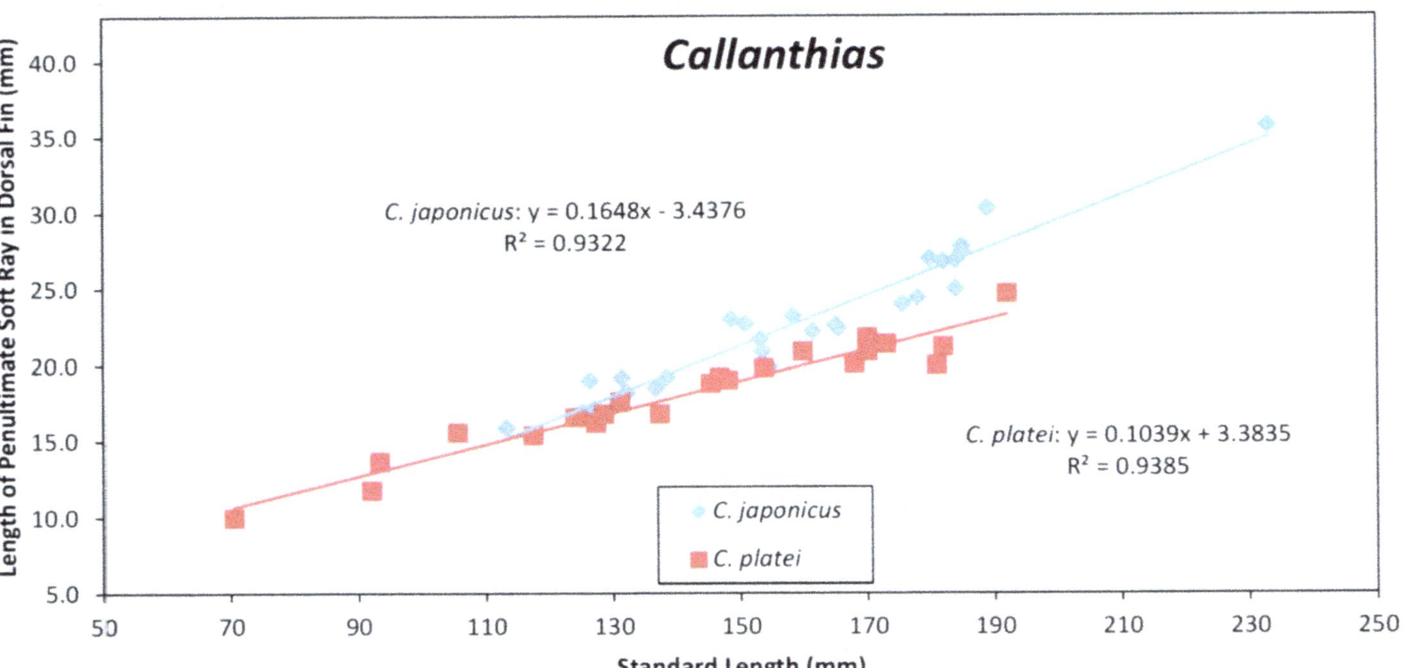

Figure 17. Comparison of length of penultimate soft ray in dorsal fin versus standard length in *Callanthias japonicus* and *C. platei.*

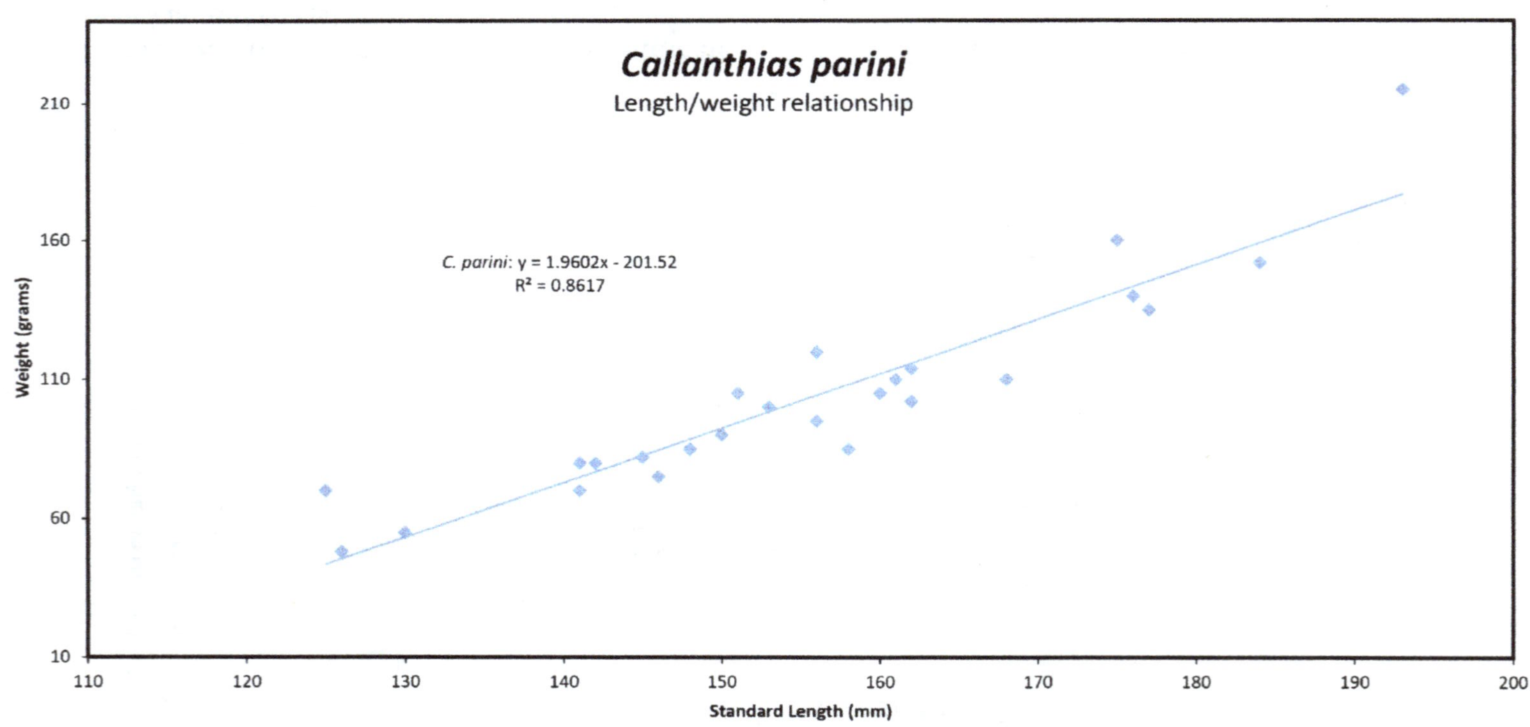

Figure 18. Standard length (mm)–weight (grams) relationship for specimens of *Callanthias parini* collected in February 1983 on the Nazca Ridge near Ecliptic Seamount.

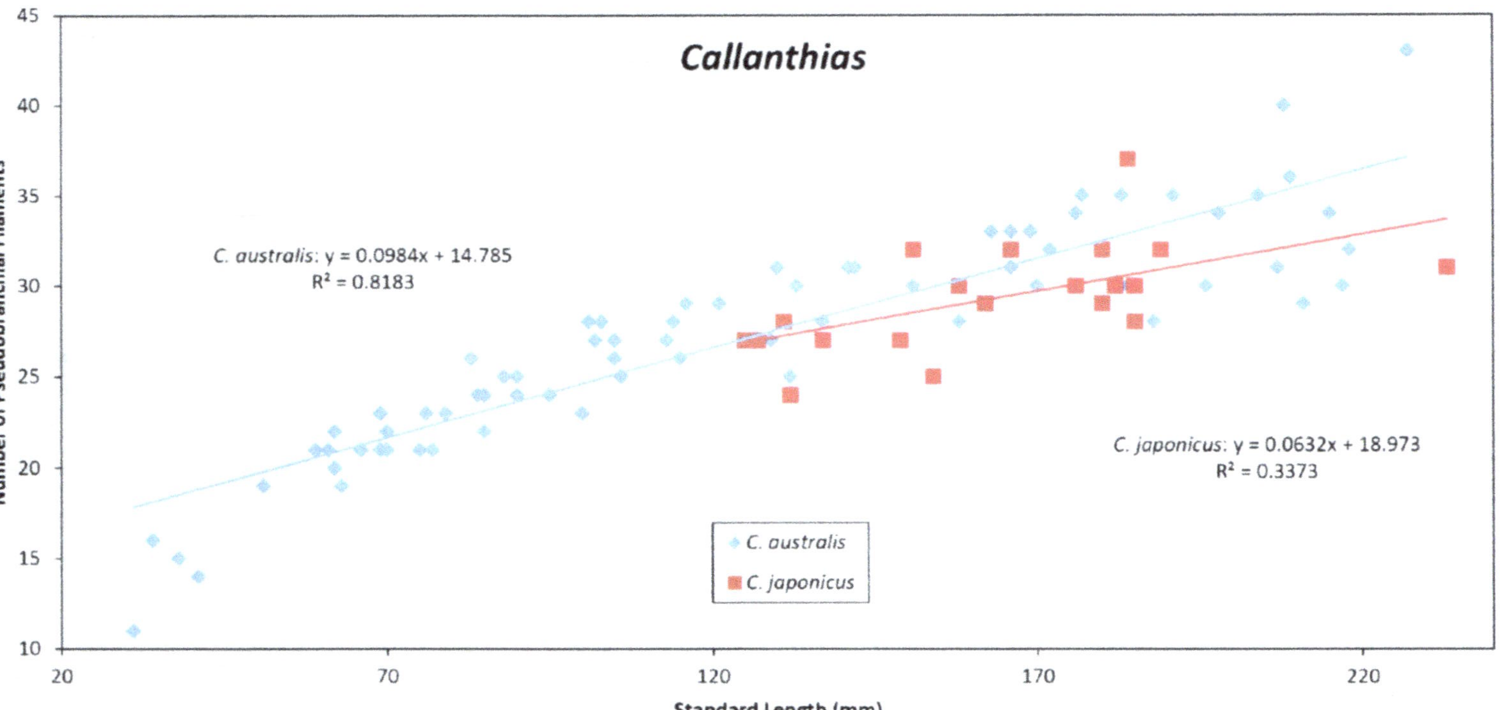

Figure 19. Relationship of number of pseudobranchial filaments to standard length in *Callanthias australis* and *C. japonicus*.

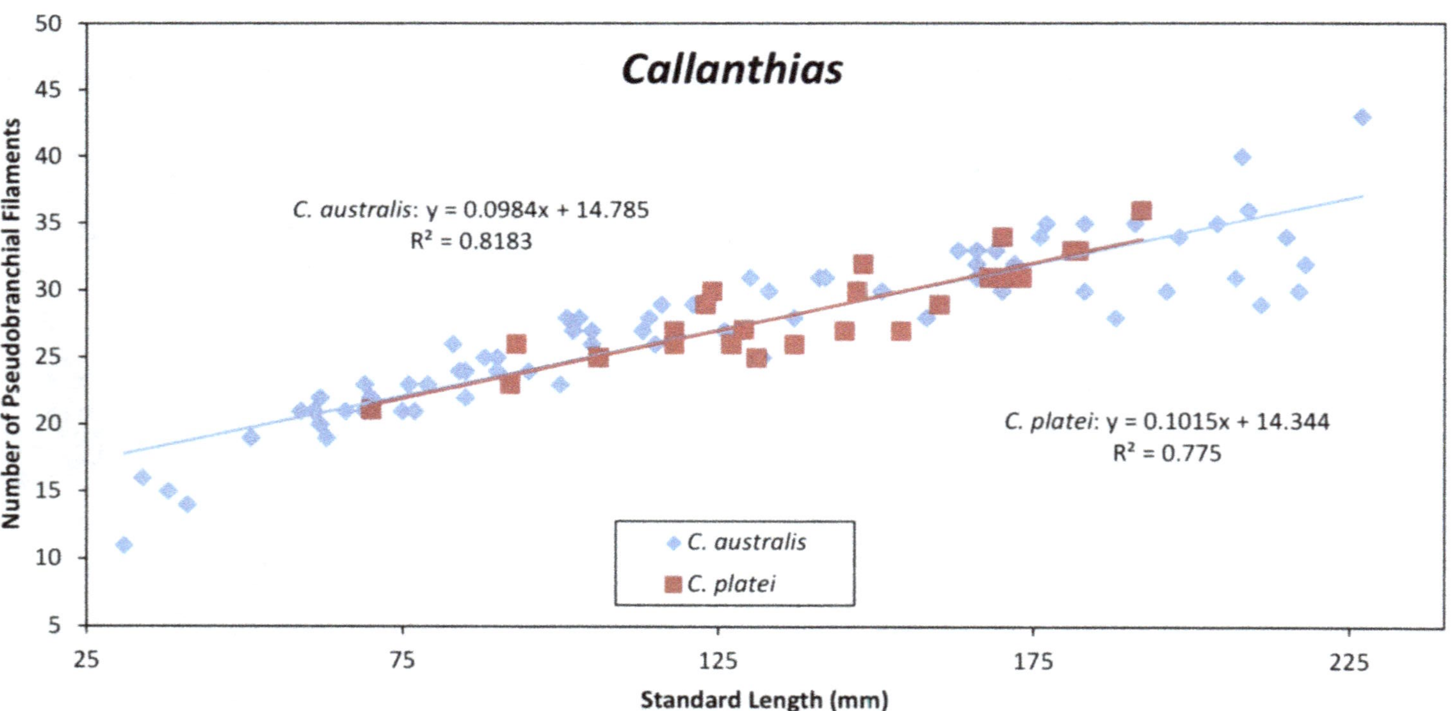

Figure 20. Relationship of number of pseudobranchial filaments to standard length in *Callanthias australis* and *C. platei*.

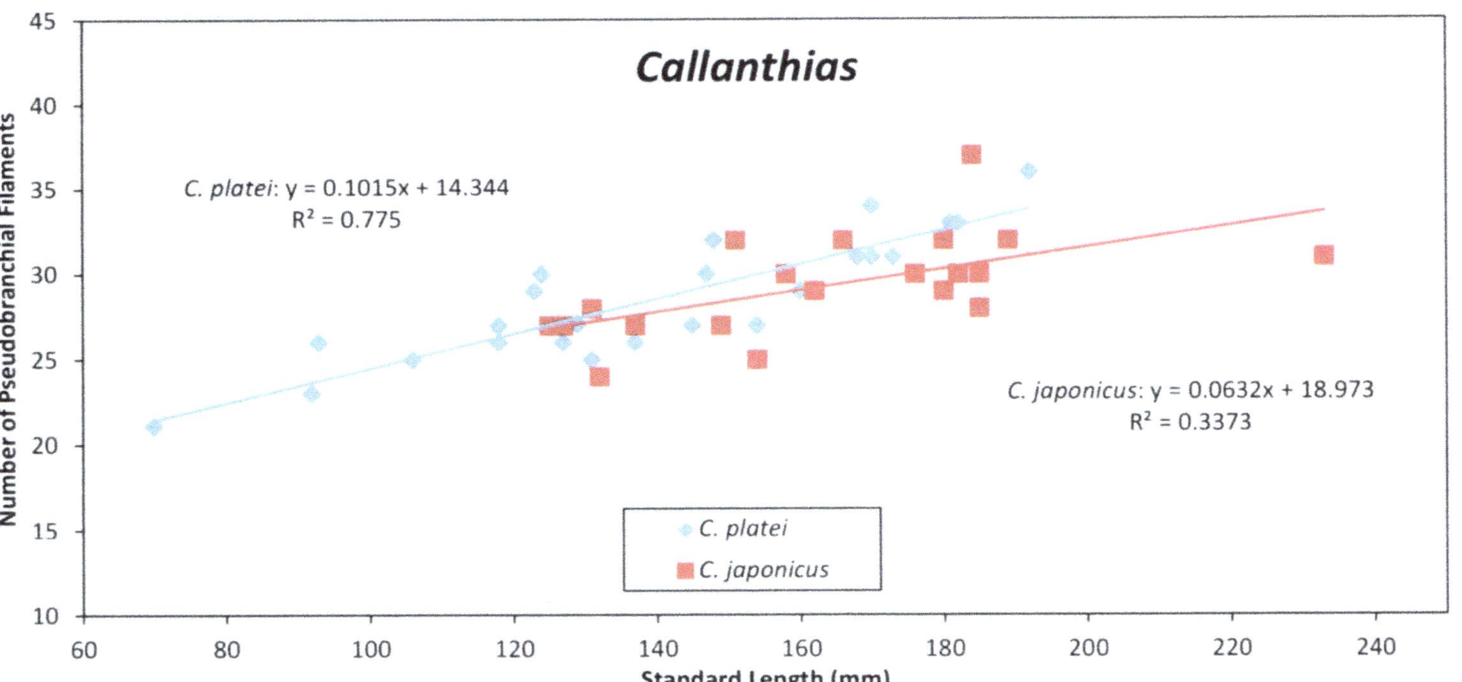

Figure 21. Relationship of number of pseudobranchial filaments to standard length in *Callanthias platei* and *C. japonicus*.

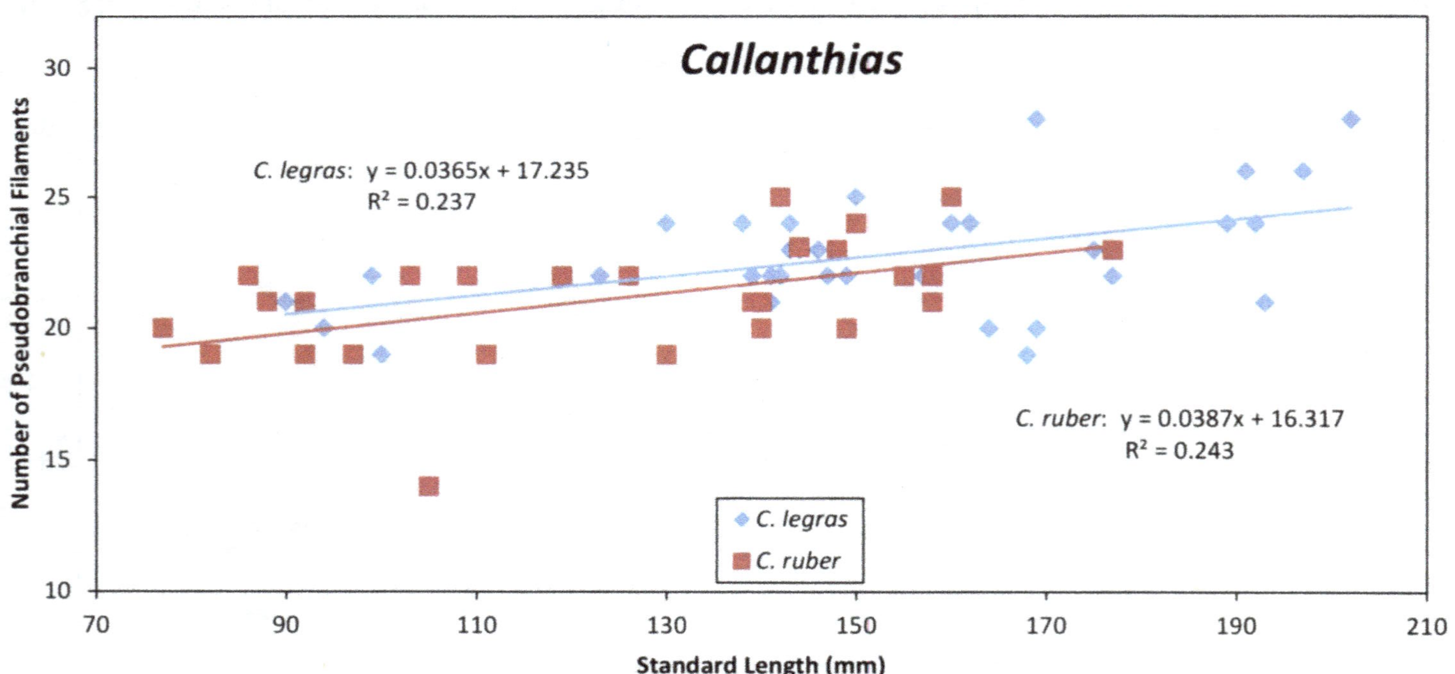

Figure 22. Relationship of number of pseudobranchial filaments to standard length in *Callanthias legras* and *C. ruber.*

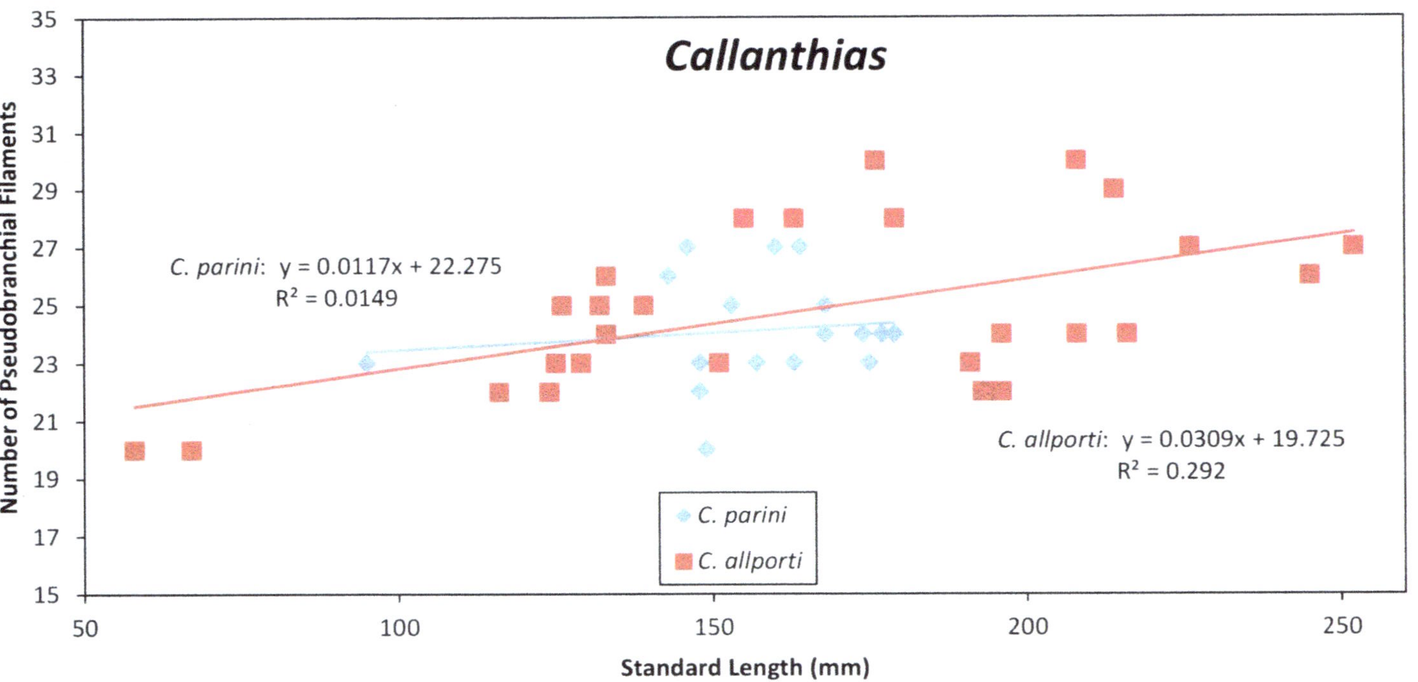

Figure 23. Relationship of number of pseudobranchial filaments to standard length in *Callanthias parini* and *C. allporti.*

TABLES

Table 1. Summary of selected characters in species of *Callanthias* (exceptional values in parentheses). H&B = present on head and body.

Characters	*allporti*	*australis*	*japonicus*	*legras*	*parini*	*platei*	*ruber*
Soft rays in dorsal fin	10	(10)11(12)	11	(9)10(11)	10	11	10(11)
Soft rays in anal fin	(9) 10	(10)11	(10)11	(9)10(11)	10	11(12)	10(11)
Pectoral-fin rays	20–23	(18,19)20–23	20--22	(18)19–20(21)	(20)21 or 22	(20) 21 or 22	(17)19–22
Total 1st arch gillrakers	30–36	(30)31–37(38)	(29)30–33	(31)32–36(38)	29–34	31–35	32–36(37)
Tubed lateral-line scales	36–47, usually 37--42	(31)34–41(42)	33–41, usually 35–39	28–36, usually 29–33	24–31, usually 26–29	(36)37–41(42)	21–25(26)
Midbody lateral scales	36–46, usually 40–43	(38,39)40–46	37–49, usually 40–46	36–42	38–46	(40)41–45(47)	34–39(40)
Total No. gillrakers plus No. lateral-line scales	(66)68–77(81)	(66)67–76(77)	65–71(72,73)	60–69(70)	(55,56)57–63	69–74(75,76)	54–60
Caudal-peduncle scales	21–25	(21)22–25	(22)23–25	15–17	21–24	(21)22–25	(18,19)20(21)
Scales between anal-fin origin and lateral line	15–19(20)	13–18 (19)	(15)16–18	12–14	(14)15–17(19)	14–17	11–14(15)
Secondary squamation	H&B, usually present	H&B, usually present	H&B, well developed	usually absent	poorly developed	H&B, well developed	absent to poorly dev.
Pseudobranch filaments	20–30	11–43, usually 21–35	24–37, usually 27–32	19–28	20–27, usually 23–27	21–36, usually 25–33	(14) 19–25
Epineurals, pairs	10–14	(11)12–14	(12)13 or 14	13–15(16)	(10, 11) 12	(12)13	11–13
Epurals	(2) 3	(2) 3	3	2(3)	(2) 3	(2) 3	3
Vomerine teeth	well developed	absent to small	small	well developed	small	absent to small	absent to small or moderate

Table 2. Frequency distributions for numbers of soft rays in the dorsal fin in species of *Callanthias.*

Species	9	10	11	12
allporti		35		
australis		1	103	2
japonicus			28	
legras	2	43	1	
parini		19		
platei			26	
ruber		49	1	

Table 3. Frequency distributions for numbers of soft rays in the anal fin in species of *Callanthias.*

Species	9	10	11	12
allporti	1	35		
australis		2	105	
japonicus		1	27	
legras	1	44	1	
parini		19		
platei			25	1
ruber		48	2	

Table 4. Frequency distributions for numbers of rays in the pectoral fin in species of *Callanthias*.

Species	17	18	19	20	21	22	23
allporti—left				5	17	13	1
allporti—right				3	15	14	2
australis—left			1	2	39	39	6
australis—right		1	—	3	38	40	4
japonicus—left				3	24	1	
japonicus—right				4	22	2	
legras—left		2	24	19	1		
legras—right		1	19	22	1		
parini—left					6	13	
parini—right				1	6	12	
platei—left				2	18	5	
platei—right				2	19	5	
ruber—left	1	—	2	15	27	3	
ruber—right			1	12	32	4	

Table 5. Frequency distributions for sums of numbers of pectoral-fin rays from left and right sides of individual specimens in species of *Callanthias*.

No. of rays	*allporti*	*australis*	*japonicus*	*legras*	*parini*	*platei*	*ruber*
37				3			
38				17			2
39				5			1
40	2	2	2	17		2	11
41	2	3	3	—		—	4
42	15	32	21	1	6	17	25
43	3	8	1		2	2	3
44	9	34	1		11	4	2
45	3	2					
46		4					

Table 6. Frequency distributions for total numbers of gillrakers (GR) on first arch in species of *Callanthias*.

No. of GR	*allporti*	*australis*	*japonicus*	*legras*	*parini*	*platei*	*ruber*
29			1		2		
30	3	1	4		2		
31	4	2	8	2	4	6	
32	6	9	10	5	3	6	5
33	11	18	3	13	4	10	8
34	7	32		11	1	2	11
35	2	13		8		2	20
36	2	6		3			4
37		2		—			1
38		1		1			

Table 7. Frequency distributions for numbers of tubed lateral-line scales (LL) in species of *Callanthias*. Counts from both sides. Left side presented first.

LL scales	*allporti*	*australis*	*japonicus*	*legras*	*parini*	*platei*	*ruber*
21							1, 3
22							8, 6
23							28, 25
24					__, 1		6, 5
25					1, 1		2, 5
26					6, 6		__, 1
27					1, 4		
28				2, 2	5, 1		
29				3, 8	3, 4		
30				10, 7	1, __		
31		__, 1		8, 7	1, __		
32		__		7, 8			
33		__	__, 1	5, 4			
34		1, 3	__, 2	1, 1			
35		2, 12	3, __	2, 3			
36	1, 1	23, 18	6, 7	1, 1		1, 1	
37	2, 4	23, 19	10, 5			1, 3	
38	5, 3	21, 22	5, 5			8, 4	
39	5, 9	14, 7	1, 3			4, 9	
40	5, 3	6, 6	1, 1			4, 4	
41	5, 8	2, 4	1, 1			7, 3	
42	5, __	__, 1				__, 1	
43	1, 1						
44	1, __						
45	__						
46	__						
47	1, __						

Table 8. Frequency distributions for sums of numbers of tubed lateal-line scales (LL) from left and right sides in individual specimens of species of *Callanthias*.

Number of LL scales	*allporti*	*australis*	*japonicus*	*legras*	*parini*	*platei*	*ruber*
43							2
44							3
45							7
46							17
47							5
48							4
49							2
50					1		2
51					1		
52					3		
53					2		
54					2		
55					1		
56					2		
57				1	1		
58				4	1		
59				3	1		
60				6	1		
61				1			
62				6			
63				5			
64				2			
65				3			
66				1			
67				1			
68			1	1			
69		2	—	—			
70		3	2	2			
71		5	1	1			
72		9	2				
73		8	5			1	
74	2	16	1			—	
75	1	15	4			3	
76	2	10	3			2	
77	1	7	2			4	
78	5	5	2			2	
79	3	1	—			4	
80	3	3	1			2	
81	4	2				3	
82	3	—				2	
83	3	1				1	

Table 9. Frequency distributions for numbers of lateral-line scales posterior to base of ultimate dorsal soft ray in species of *Callanthias*. L = left side, R = right side. –1 or –2 means that lateral line (LL) terminates either 1 or 2 scales anterior to posterior end of soft dorsal fin. TBCF = lateral line terminates at base of caudal fin.

LL scales	*allporti*	*australis*	*japonicus*	*legras*	*parini*	*platei*	*ruber*
–2							1 R
–1					1 L, 3 R		1 L
0					13 L, 2 R		8 L, 7 R
1				1 R	5L, 4 R		14 L, 14 R
2		1 R		2 L, 1 R	—		2 L, 3 R
3		—		6 L, 11 R	1 R		
4		—	1 R	10 L, 12 R			
5	1 R	2 R	—	9 L, 3 R			
6	2 L, 1 R	4 L, 3 R	2 L	7 L, 5 R			
7	4 L, 3 R	6 L, 7, R	3 R	2 L, 4 R			
8	7 L, 12 R	19 L, 18 R	5 L, 7 R	1 L, 1 R			
9	14 L, 11 R	28 L, 24 R	13 L, 5 R	1 L		2 L, 2 R	
10	6 L, 4 R	14 L, 14 R	5 L, 6 R	1 R		4 L, 4 R	
11	1 R	3 L, 4 R	1 L, 1 R				
12	1 L	2 R					
TBCF	1 L	1 L					

Table 10. Frequency distributions for sums of numbers of gillrakers on right first arch plus numbers of tubed lateral-line scales in individual specimens of species of *Callanthias*. Sums including left side lateral-line scales presented first, followed by those for right side.

GR + LL Scales	*allporti*	*australis*	*japonicus*	*legras*	*parini*	*platei*	*ruber*
54							2, 2
55					__, 1		5, 4
56					1, __		7, 5
57					1, 2		10, 10
58					3, 4		9, 13
59					3, 2		9, 5
60				1, 2	4, 3		3, 6
61				1, __	__, __		
62				4, 6	1, 1		
63				7, 4	2, 1		
64				4, 8			
65			__, 2	6, 3			
66	__, 1	__, 2	2, 2	5, 3			
67	__, __	__, 4	5, 3	4, 5			
68	3, 3	6, 3	7, 5	4, 5			
69	__, __	9, 14	8, 3	3, 2		3, 2	
70	5, 2	17, 12	__, 4	1, 1		2, 2	
71	3, 6	12, 11	1, 2			5, 6	
72	1, 5	13, 15	1, 1			7, 12	
73	6, 4	10, 6	1,1			5, 2	
74	6, 5	5, 7				2, __	
75	4, 1	5, 4				1,__	
76	3, 1	3, 3				__, 1	
77	__, 2	__, 1					
78	__, __						
79	__, __						
80	__, __						
81	1, __						

Table 11. Frequency distributions for numbers of mid-body lateral scales in species of *Callanthias*.

Number of Scales	*allporti*	*australis*	*japonicus*	*legras*	*parini*	*platei*	*ruber*
34							3
35							1
36	1			2			7
37	—		1	3			5
38	1	1	—	5	1		6
39	1	1	—	2	1		3
40	3	10	3	4	—	1	1
41	3	8	1	3	1	4	
42	4	16	1	4	3	3	
43	6	13	2		2	5	
44	1	9	3		2	7	
45	1	9	1		1	4	
46	1	4	2		1	—	
47			—			1	
48			—				
49			1				

Table 12. Frequency distributions for numbers of circum-caudal-peduncular (CP) scales in species of *Callanthias*.

Number of CP Scales	*allporti*	*australis*	*japonicus*	*legras*	*parini*	*platei*	*ruber*
15				2			
16				16			
17				2			
18							1
19							3
20							21
21	5	1			1	1	1
22	5	3	1		1	3	
23	10	20	5		5	11	
24	6	39	9		3	7	
25	3	9	3			3	

Table 13. Frequency distributions for numbers of scales between anal-fin origin and lateral line in species of *Callanthias*.

Numbers of Scales	*allporti*	*australis*	*japonicus*	*legras*	*parini*	*platei*	*ruber*
11							3
12				6			6
13		6		12			14
14		9		6	1	4	3
15	3	17	1		2	7	1
16	1	26	6		4	13	
17	8	9	5		7	2	
18	9	4	4		—		
19	2	1			1		
20	1						

Table 14. Frequency distributions for numbers of rows of cheek scales in species of *Callanthias*.

Number of rows	*allporti*	*australis*	*japonicus*	*legras*	*parini*	*platei*	*ruber*
5		19		2			3
6	4	17	4	5		7	7
7	2	18	4	1	2	17	11
8	5	7	3	1	4	1	1
9	4		1		5		
10	2				1		

Table 15. Frequency distributions for numbers of pseudobranchial filaments in species of *Callanthias.*

Number of Filaments	*allporti*	*australis*	*japonicus*	*legras*	*parini*	*platei*	*ruber*
11		1					
12		—					
13		—					
14		1					1
15		1					—
16		1					—
17		—					—
18		—					—
19		2		2			5
20	2	1		3	1		3
21	—	7		3	—	1	5
22	4	4		9	1	—	7
23	4	5		4	5	1	3
24	4	4	1	7	4	—	1
25	3	4	1	1	2	2	2
26	2	3	—	2	1	4	
27	2	5	4	—	3	4	
28	3	6	2	2		—	
29	1	3	2			2	
30	2	6	4			2	
31		5	1			3	
32		3	4			1	
33		3	—			2	
34		3	—			1	
35		4	—			—	
36		1	—			1	
37		—	1				
38		—					
39		—					
40		1					
41		—					
42		—					
43		1					

Table 16. Frequency distributions for numbers of procurrent caudal-fin rays in species of *Callanthias.*

Number of fin rays	*allporti*	*australis*	*japonicus*	*legras*	*parini*	*platei*	*ruber*
Dorsal							
6				20			1
7	19	1	1	24	12	1	28
8	16	63	20	1	6	10	17
9		20	5			13	
Ventral							
5				1			
6	7			31			8
7	21	19	7	13	18	3	36
8	6	59	17			13	4
9		6	3			9	

Table 17. Frequency distributions for numbers of epineural and epural bones and trisegmental pterygiophores in species of *Callanthias*.

Number of bones	*allporti*	*australis*	*japonicus*	*legras*	*parini*	*platei*	*ruber*
Epineurals (pairs)							
10	4				1		
11	12	1			2		13
12	10	6	1		13	3	12
13	3	47	20	3		16	8
14	2	22	7	16			
15				17			
16				1			
Epurals							
2	1	5		45	2	1	
3	34	85	28	1	17	25	48
Dorsal trisegmental pterygiophores							
0							1
1	26	64	27	19	16	20	33
2	1			2			
Anal trisegmental pterygiophores							
0							1
1	27	71	28	18	17	23	34
2				2			

Table 18. Comparisons of morphometric data in four species of *Callanthias* that usually have 10 soft rays in both dorsal and anal fins; standard length (SL) in mm, other measurements in % SL.

	Callanthias allporti		***Callanthias legras***		***Callanthias parini***		***Callanthias ruber***	
	n	**RANGES**	**n**	**RANGES**	**n**	**Ranges**	**n**	**RANGES**
SL	34	57.9-252	40	90.2-202	19	39.6-179	36	76.8-177
Depth@DFO	33	29.2-38.8	40	25.9-33.3	18	27.5-36.9	34	24.2-30.6
Predorsal lgth	34	26.5-35.1	30	27.9-36.7	18	29.1-33.7	36	26.0-30.9
Head lgth	33	25.1-32.0	40	26.7-31.9	19	28.8-36.6	36	25.9-31.2
Snout lgth	32	5.2-7.8	32	5.2-9.6	19	5.7-8.4	36	4.5-6.8
Orbit diam.	33	7.9-13.8	32	8.6-11.2	19	10.8-15.4	36	9.1-14.5
Interorbital	34	5.5-9.4	30	7.2-9.0	18	6.3-8.7	36	6.5-8.7
Postorbital	33	10.5-13.4	32	11.4-13.9	19	11.9-15.7	36	10.4-13.4
Upperjawlgth	34	11.9-14.9	30	11.7-13.8	18	12.1-15.4	36	12.0-14.5
Pect. fin lgth	32	21.3-27.5	29	22.7-26.7	17	23.8-28.3	27	20.1-24.5
Pelv. fin lgth	31	22.3-31.5	21	23.1-31.6	17	20.9-25.4	31	22.4-27.1
Lgth caudped	34	19.0-26.9	30	21.0-25.6	19	18.8-22.8	36	20.0-24.8
Dpth caudped	34	10.4-16.7	30	11.7-14.2	18	10.0-12.6	36	10.5-14.0
Up. caud lobe	22	30.6-85.3	20	26.0-34.7	10	29.7-60.3	17	34.2-71.6+
Lo. caud lobe	21	28.7-72.4	23	24.7-32.6	14	27.4-69.3	20	35.5-85.5
A. fin length	32	37.1-47.7	36	38.4-64.9	18	35.7-51.2	33	39.5-46.7
1st anal spine	29	6.3-10.8	28	2.8-6.2	15	5.7-9.9	30	5.7-9.2
2nd anal spine	28	10.7-17.6	28	6.3-9.8	14	9.7-21.9	28	7.5-13.0
3rd anal spine	29	13.3-19.6	29	9.0-13.7+	16	12.9-26.0+	28	10.5-15.4
Anal base lgth	34	24.5-30.5	29	21.2-26.6	18	23.0-28.8	36	24.0-29.5
Penult D ray	30	13.3-19.2	35	14.5-23.3	16	13.1-24.6	30	15.3-19.8
Ult D ray	29	11.7-16.8	33	11.1-15.9	17	10.8-23.5	29	12.3-17.4
Penult A ray	29	13.1-17.7	34	11.0-20.2	16	14.0-25.6	29	15.5-21.4
Ult A ray	30	11.7-17.6	33	10.0-15.9	15	12.5-23.9	29	14.2-19.5

Table 19. Comparisons of morphometric data in three species of *Callanthias* that usually have 11 soft rays in both dorsal and anal fins. Standard length in mm, other measurements in % SL.

	Callanthias platei		***Callanthias japonicus***		***Callanthias australis***	
	n	**Range**	**n**	**Range**	**n**	**Range**
Standard length	26	70.5-192	28	113-233	85	30.6-227
Depth at dorsal-fin origin	25	27.3-32.0	28	28.9-34.7	84	25.7-35.7
Predorsal length	26	25.5-29.9	28	27.7-31.8	85	26.1-34.1
Head length	26	22.3-26.7	28	24.1-28.4	85	24.4-31.0
Snout length	26	4.9-6.6	28	5.2-7.1	85	4.7-7.2
Orbit diameter	26	6.5-9.5	28	7.9-9.5	85	7.6-13.1
Interorbital width	26	6.1-8.8	28	6.0-8.7	83	5.7-9.1
Postorbital length	26	9.7-12.4	28	10.3-12.3	85	9.6-12.0
Upper-jaw length	26	9.1-11.1	28	11.1-12.4	84	10.0-13.7
Pectoral-fin length	26	18.6-24.5	27	20.4-24.0	79	20.8-25.3
Pelvic-fin length	25	20.1-24.4	27	20.8-26.1	76	20.4-25.9
Length of caudal peduncle	26	17.2-22.4	28	17.1-21.3	85	16.3-21.1
Depth of caudal peduncle	26	11.0-13.4	28	12.1-14.4	84	10.8-14.1
Upper caudal-fin lobe	24	26.2-69.4+	17	33.4-53.7	37	30.0-71.9
Lower caudal-fin lobe	25	26.0-63.7+	19	30.2-54.5+	51	27.0-70.0
Anal-fin length	26	39.9-45.7	28	39.8-46.1	79	38.5-49.8
1st anal-spine length	23	6.0-8.4	27	6.7-9.4+	64	6.5-11.1
2nd anal-spine length	25	8.0-10.8	23	9.0-13.9	65	9.2-13.8
3rd anal-spine length	24	9.1-13.2	24	10.4-15.0	55	10.5-15.1
Anal-fin, base length	26	28.5-33.3	28	27.2-35.8	85	27.6-35.7
Penultimate dorsal-fin ray	25	11.0-14.8	28	12.9-16.0	76	11.2-18.0
Ultimate dorsal-fin ray	23	10.3-13.5	28	11.9-13.9	73	10.2-16.1
Penultimate anal-fin ray	24	11.4-14.2	28	12.2-14.6	79	10.5-17.5
Ultimate anal-fin ray	25	10.1-13.5	28	11.4-14.0	78	8.6-15.7

Table 20. *Callanthias:* all seven species--dimorphisms (trimorphism in *C. australis*); standard length in mm, other measurements in % SL.

Callanthias allporti				
	Short Caudal-fin Lobes		Long Caudal-fin Lobes	
	n	RANGE	n	RANGE
Standard length	9	57.9-176	16	114-252
Upper caudal lobe	9	30.6-43.6+	13	49.0-85.3
Lower caudal lobe	7	28.7-44.0	14	51.1-72.4
Ultimate anal soft ray	7	11.7-14.7	16	13.4-17.6

Callanthias australis						
	Short caudal-fin lobes		Medium caudal-fin lobes		Long caudal-fin lobes	
	n	RANGE	n	RANGE	n	RANGE
Standard length	39	41.1-217	14	69.0-211	3	171-227
Body, depth@DFO	39	26.1-34.4	14	28.1-33.0	3	33.9-35.7
Upper caudal lobe	22	30.0-38.5	11	36.1-45.3	3	64.3+-71.9
Lower caudal lobe	37	27.0-37.2	10	31.6-47.7	3	56.6+-70.0

Callanthias australis				
	Short caudal-fin lobes		Long caudal-fin lobes	
	n	RANGE	n	RANGE
Standard length	53	41.1-217	3	171-227
Upper caudal lobe	33	30.0-45.3	3	64.3+-71.9
Lower caudal lobe	47	27.0-47.7	3	56.6+-70.0

Callanthias japonicus				
	Short caudal-fin lobes		Long caudal-fin lobes	
	n	RANGE	n	RANGE
Standard length	17	113-184	7	153-233
Upper caudal lobe	11	33.4-40.9	6	43.7-53.7
Lower caudal lobe	13	30.2-36.9	6	43.2-54.5+
Anal fin, base length	17	27.2-31.8	7	30.1-35.8

Table 20. (*continued*)

Callanthias legras				
	Short anal fin		**Long anal fin**	
	n	**RANGE**	**n**	**RANGE**
Standard length	14	90.2-170	22	100-202
Lower caudal lobe	8	24.7-30.0	13	27.6-32.6
Anal-fin length	14	38.4-44.1	21	45.1-64.9
Penult. dorsal soft ray	14	14.6-17.9	20	14.5-23.3
Penult. anal soft ray	13	11.0-16.7	20	14.8-20.2

Callanthias platei				
	Short caudal-fin lobes		**Long caudal-fin lobes**	
	n	**RANGE**	**n**	**RANGE**
Standard length	18	70.5-181	8	137-192
Upper caudal lobe	17	26.2-38.0+	8	46.7+-69.4+
Lower caudal lobe	16	26.0-35.7+	8	50.2+-63.7+

Callanthias ruber				
	Short caudal-fin lobes		**Long caudal-fin lobes**	
	n	**RANGE**	**n**	**RANGE**
Standard length	3	81.5-126	17	111-177
Upper caudal lobe	2	34.2-42.6	15	44.4+- 71.6+
Lower caudal lobe	3	35.5-39.8	17	49.7+-85.5

Table 20. (*continued*)

	Callanthias parini			
	Short fins and fin rays		**Long fins and fin rays**	
	n	**RANGE**	**n**	**RANGE**
Standard length	8	68.0-157	10	149-179
2nd dorsal spine	3	6.9-7.6	7	7.7-10.5
3rd dorsal spine	3	9.0-10.1	5	11.7-14.9
5th dorsal spine	3	10.4-12.4	5	17.1-18.4
7th dorsal spine	3	11.8-15.2	4	22.2-23.0
9th dorsal spine	3	14.0-16.6	1	26.1
11th dorsal spine	2	14.5-16.8	3	27.2-27.7
1st dorsal soft ray	3	17.7-19.5	6	29.6-ca. 32.6
3rd dorsal soft ray	3	18.5-19.3	6	ca. 29.7- 32.1
7th dorsal soft ray	3	16.4-17.8	7	23.6-27.1
Penultimate dorsal soft ray	7	13.1-15.7	10	18.6-24.6
Ultimate dorsal soft ray	7	10.8-13.8	10	16.8-23.5
Dorsal-fin length	3	66.1-66.4	7	72.3-79.9
1st anal spine	8	5.7-7.7	8	7.1-9.9
2nd anal spine	6	9.7-13.3	8	17.2-21.9
3rd anal spine	8	12.9-15.4	8	20.7->26.0
1st anal soft ray	2	16.4-17.4	6	25.8-28.7
3rd anal soft ray	2	17.1-18.5	7	28.6-30.5
4th anal soft ray	3	17.5-19.0	7	29.0-31.2
Penultimate anal soft ray	6	14.0-15.5	10	18.6-25.6
Ultimate anal soft ray	6	12.5-13.9	10	17.9-23.9
Anal-fin length	8	35.7-43.2	10	44.5-51.2
Upper caudal lobe	7	29.7-33.4	3	ca. 44.1-60.3
Lower caudal lobe	8	27.4-ca. 32.3	6	ca. 33.2-69.3

MAPS

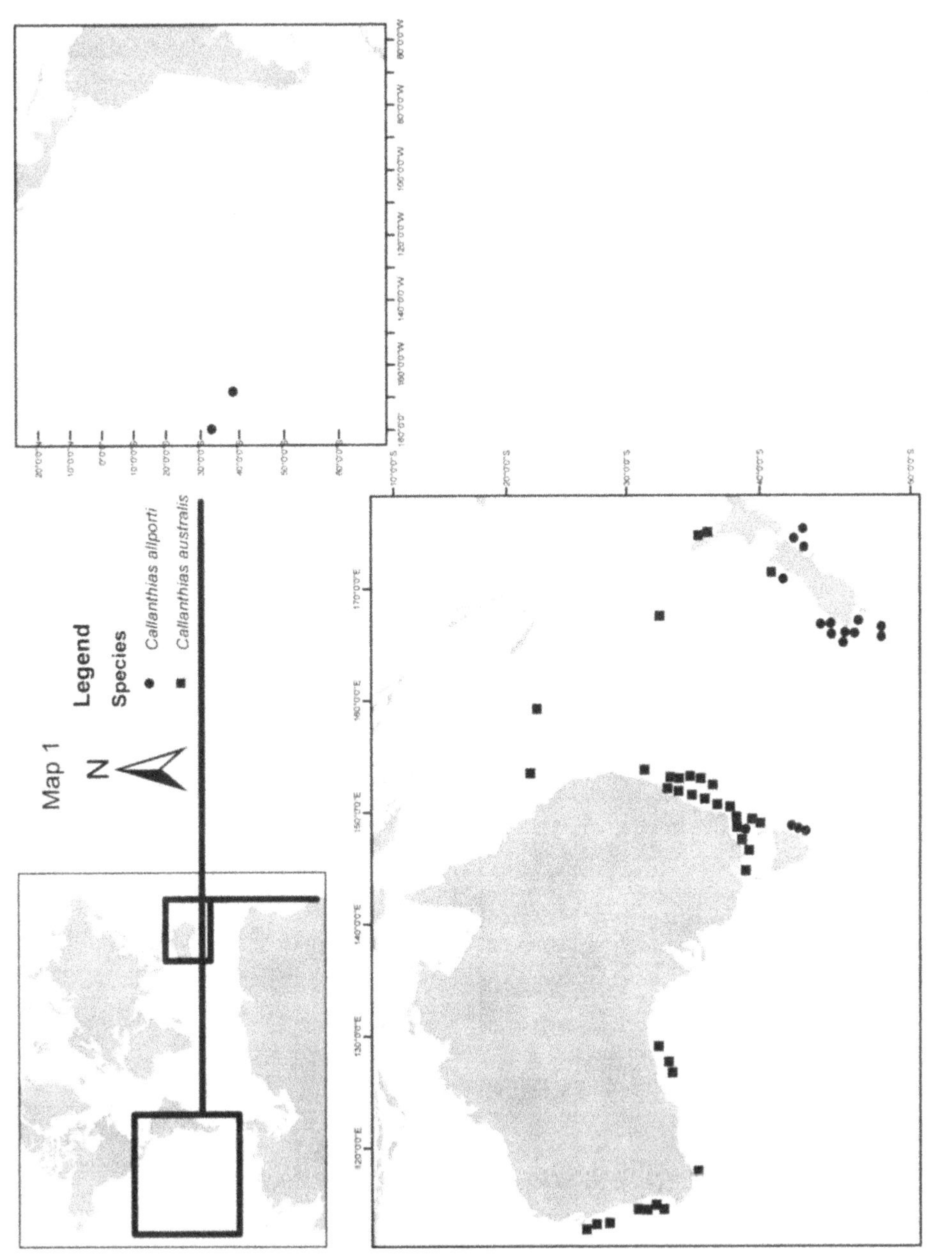

Map 1
N
Legend
Species
Callanthias allporti
Callanthias australis

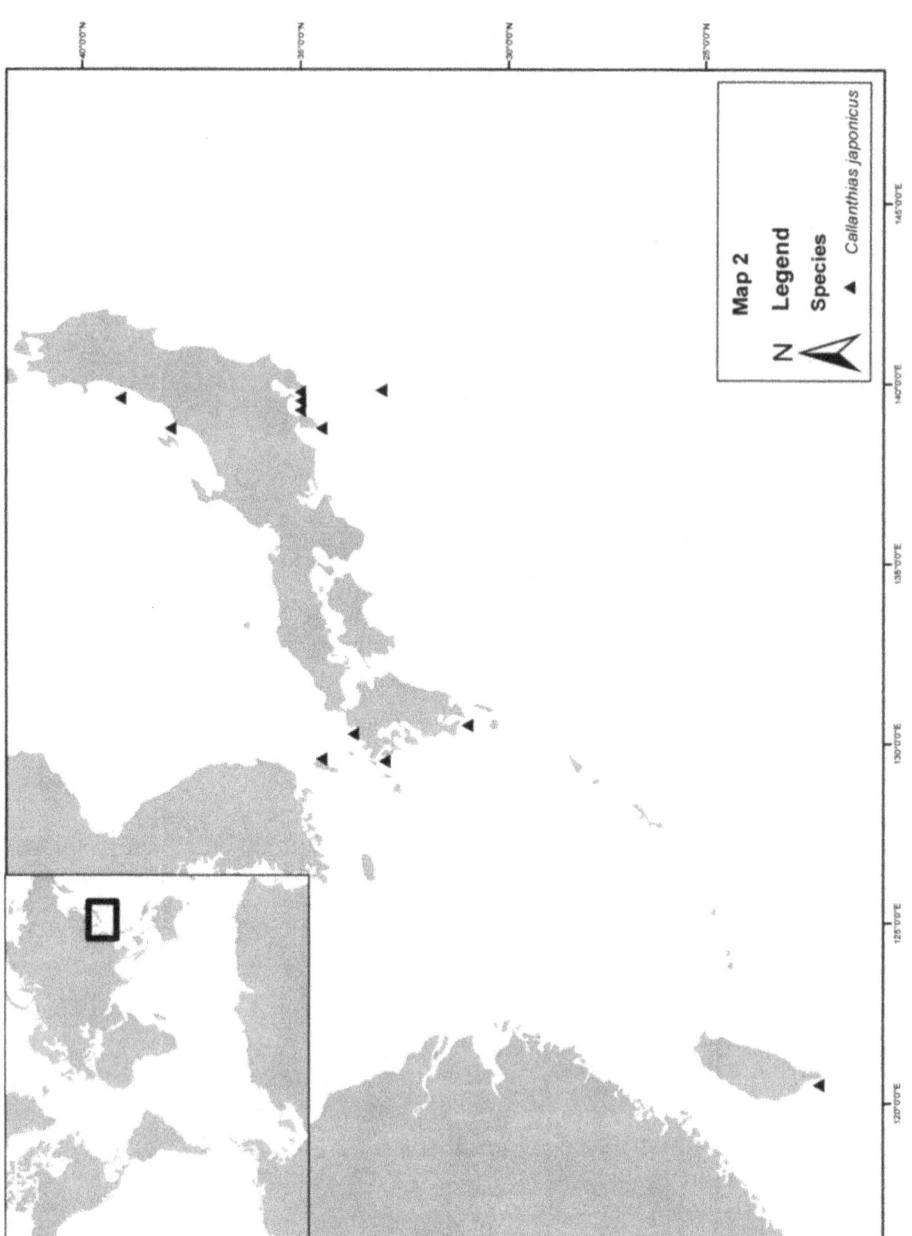
Map 2
N
Legend
Species
Callanthias japonicus

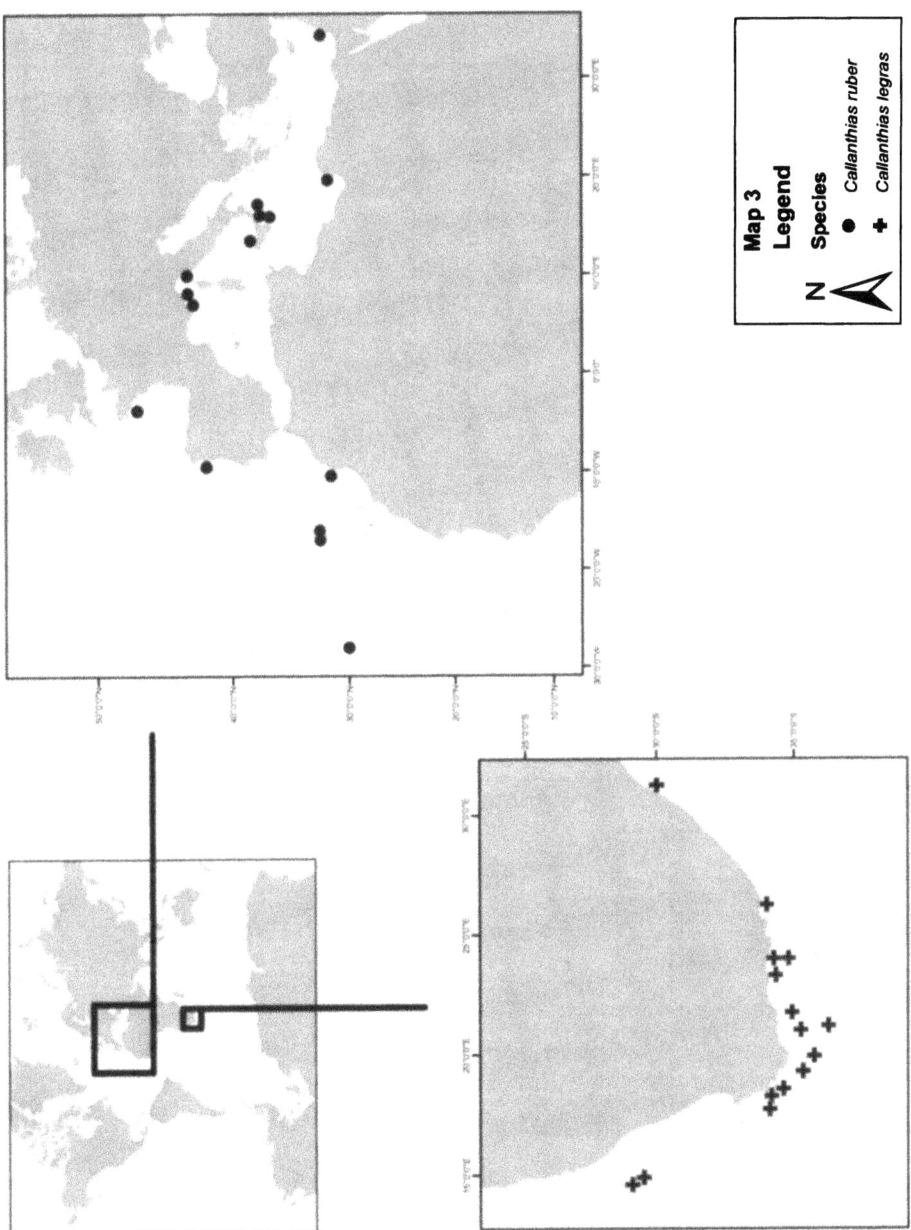
Map 3
Legend
Species
Callanthias ruber
Callanthias legras
N

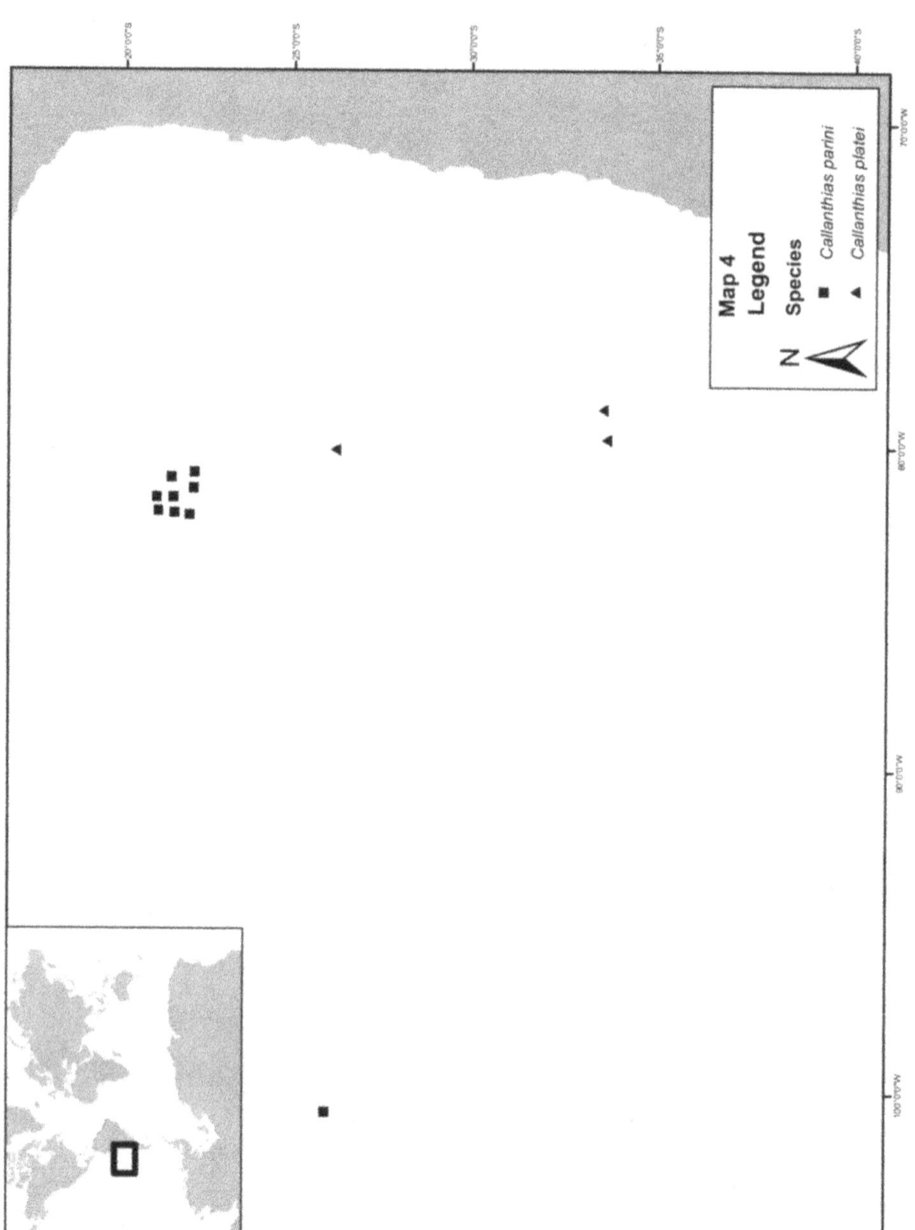
Map 4
Legend
Species
Callanthias parini
Callanthias platei
N

Map 5: *Callanthias* species of the world

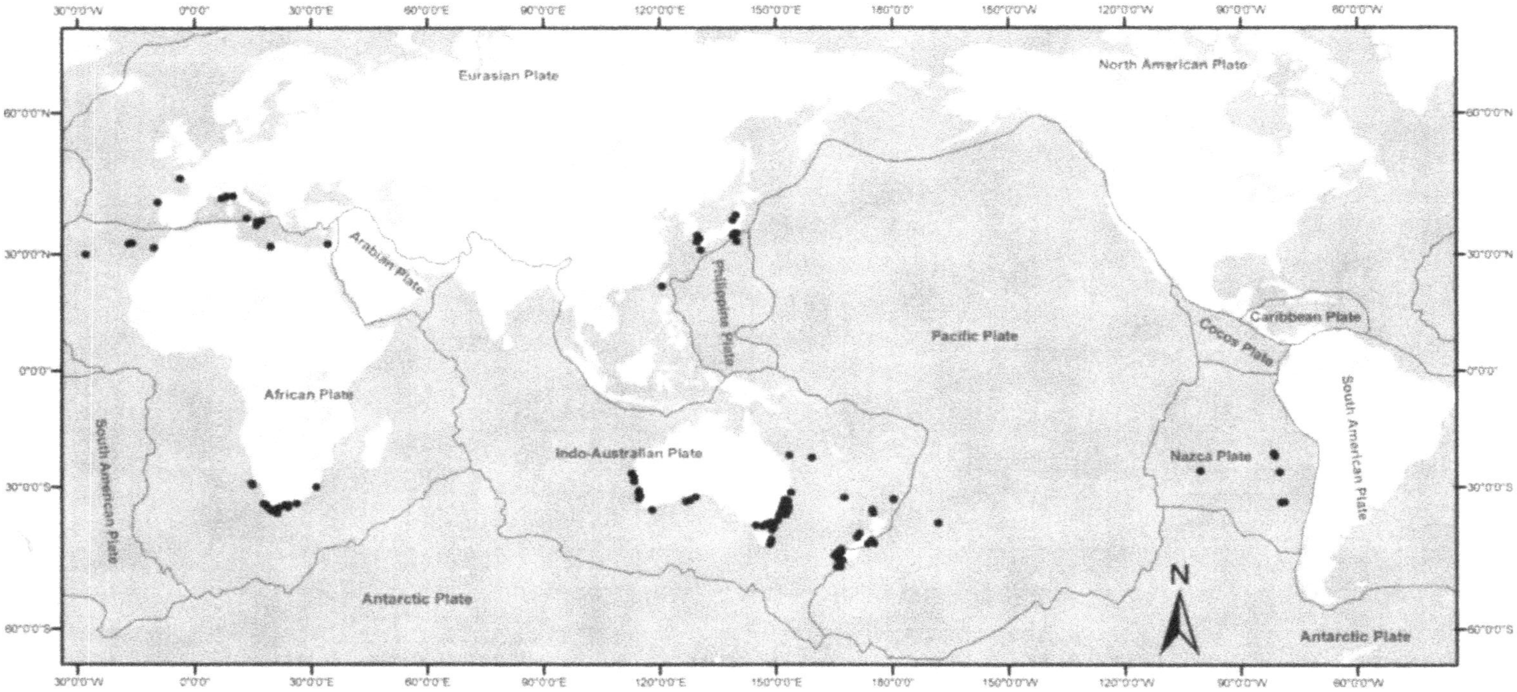

INDEX

KEY

Species of *Callanthias*, 11–12

SCIENTIFIC NAMES

Acipenser, 46
Amia calva, 46
Anogramma, 5
Anthias
  A. buphthalmos, 41, 44
  A. noeli, 47
Anthiinae, 1, 27, 51
Anthiine serranid, 14, 21, 39, 47
Aulostomus chinensis, 50
Aulostomus strigosus, 50
Batrachoididae, 49
Bodianus peloritanus, 41
Caesioperca lepidoptera, 14, 21
Callanthias
  C. allporti, ii, xi, xiv, xvii, 5, 8, 11, 13–15, 19, 21, 22, 47, 51, 65, 95
  C. australis, xi, xiii, xiv, xvi, xvii, 8, 9, 11, 13, 15, 17–23, 27, 45, 47, 49, 66, 73, 74, 78, 79, 80, 81, 82, 83, 84, 85, 91, 92
  C. japonicus, xi, xiii, xiv, xvii, 5, 8, 11, 17, 18, 25–27, 45, 47, 56, 63, 75, 77, 78, 79, 80, 81, 86, 87, 88, 89, 91, 93
  C. legras, xi, xiv, xvii, 6, 8, 11, 94
  C. paradisaeus, 5, 41, 44, 71
  C. parini, xi, xiv, xvii, 8, 9, 11, 33–35, 46, 47, 49, 69, 90, 95
  C. peloritanus, 41, 42, 43, 61
  C. platei, xi, xiii, xiv, xvii, 12, 17, 18, 22, 25, 37–40, 82, 83, 84, 85, 86, 87, 88, 89, 92, 93
  C. platei australis, 17, 19
  C. ruber, xi, xiv, xvii, 5, 11, 41–44, 47, 53, 62, 71, 94
  C. sp., xi, 33, 72
  C. splendens, 17, 19–20, 22, 66
"Callanthiida" excavate, 42
"?Callanthiida" sulcata, 42
Callanthiidae, xix, 1, 2, 49, 51, 52, 55, 56, 57, 59, 62
Callanthiinae, 1, 8
Canthigaster, 50, 57
Caprodon, 39
  Caprodon longimanus, 21
Gramma, 1, 48
Grammatidae, 1, 54
Grammatonotus, xix, 1, 2, 5, 45, 48, 56, 57
  G. crosnieri, 74
  G. laysanus, 5, 42, 75
  G. macrophthalmus, 45
Lepimphis ruber, 41
Lepisosteus osseus, 46
Lipogramma, 1
Micropterus salmoides, 73
Opistognathidae, 49
Parabarossia, 2
Percanthias, 5
Pomatomidae, 49
Pristidae, 49
Rachycentridae, 49
Sciaenidae, 49
Serranidae, 1, 2, 8, 51, 52, 54, 55, 56, 57, 62
Sillaginidae, 49
Symphysanodon, 50, 52

VERNACULAR NAMES

African Goldie, 29
African Splendid Perch, 29
Allport's Groppo, 13
Bird-of-Paradise Fish, 41
Butterfly Perch, 14
Eastern Atlantic Groppo, 41
Glorious Groppo, 17
Goldie/Goldies, 5, 17
Groppos, 5
Japanese Goldie, 25
Japanese Splendid Perch, 25
Juan Fernández Spendid Perch, 37
Matulic Silioglavic, 41
Nazca Splendid Perch, 33
Northern Splendid Perch, 17, 18
Papagaio, 41
Parin's Groppo, 33
Parrot Seaperch, 41
Petunia Groppo, 25
Rosy Perch, 13
San Félix Groppo, 37
Southern Goldie, 13
Southern Splendid Perch, 13, 14
Splendid Perches, 5

LOCALITIES

Adriatic Sea, 11, 43
Aegean Sea, 11, 43
Africa
  South, 29
  southern, 11, 50
Angola, 44
Atlantic Ocean
  eastern, 51
  eastern North, 11
  eastern South, 11
  South, 50
  southeastern, 30
Australia
  northwestern, 27, 45, 54
  south-east, 55
  southern, 22, 23, 60
  western, 22, 23, 45
Australian/New Zealand region, 11, 13, 15, 17, 21
Azores, 43, 44, 52, 60
Bass Strait, 15, 22, 53
Canary Islands, 43, 53
  Tenerife, 43, 52
Chatham Rise, 15
Chesterfield Islands, 22
Coral Sea, 22
Desventuradas Islands, 12, 39, 46, 53, 59, 72
  San Felix Island, 12, 39, 40
East China Sea, 27
Emperor Seamounts, 27
England
  southern, 42
English Channel, 43
France
  Basque coast, 44
  Bay of Biscay, 44
  Nice, 42
Hawaii, 27, 42, 52
Hawaiian Archipelago, 45, 53, 57
Indian Ocean, 9
  eastern, 45
  northern, 50
  southeastern, 11
  southwestern, 30, 31
  western, 11, 61
Indonesian/Australian region, 45
Israel, 44
Italy, 44, 71
Japan, 27, 62
  Sagami Sea, Aburatsubo, 25
  Sea of Japan, 27
  Tokai Aquarium, 26, 67
Johnston Atoll, 45, 53, 59
Juan Fernández Islands, 12, 37, 39, 59
  Robinson Crusoe Island, 38, 70
Korea, 62
  southern, 27
Libya, 44
Madeira, 41, 43, 44, 57, 71

Map 1
  Callanthias allporti, 117
  Callanthias australis, 117
Map 2
  Callanthias japonicus, 118
Map 3
  Callanthias legras, 119
  Callanthias ruber, 119
Map 4
  Callanthias parini, 120
  Callanthias platei, 120
Map 5
  Callanthias species of the world, 121
Mauritania, 43
Mediterranean Sea, 11, 43, 44, 62
  eastern, 43, 54
  France
    Nice, 42
  Sicily
    Messina, 41
    Palermo, 41
  western, 41
Morocco, 44
Namibia, 30, 31
Nazca Ridge, 33, 35, 69
  Ecliptic Seamount, 34, 90
New Caledonia, 22
New South Wales, 15, 57, 63
  Norah Head, 17, 19, 22
  Port Jackson, 17, 19, 22, 66
  Port Macquarie, 22
  Sydney Market, 19
New Zealand
  Chatham Islands, 15
  Fiordland, ii, 14
  Hauraki Gulf, Auckland, 17, 20, 66
  Kermadec Islands, 22
  North Cape, 15, 22
  North Island, 15, 22
  Poor Knights Islands, 22
  Snares Islands, 15
  South Island
    Oamaru, Otago, 15
  Three Kings Islands, 22
Okinawa Trough, 27, 63
Pacific Ocean
  eastern South, 11, 12, 50
  South, 15, 22
  southeastern, 39
  western, 11
  western North, 11
  western South, 11
Queensland, 22
Ryukyu Islands, 27, 61
Sagami Sea, 25, 27, 60
Sala y Gómez Ridge, 11, 34, 35, 58, 59
San Félix Island, 12, 39, 40
Seamounts
  Ecliptic, 34
  Emperor
    Koko, 27
    Milwaukee, 27
  Great Meteor, 44, 62
Sea of Japan, 27, 56, 61
Sicily
  Messina, 41, 53
  Palermo, 41, 59
South Africa
  Algoa Bay, 29, 68
  KwaZulu-Natal, 31
  Northern Cape Province, 31
  Port Elizabeth, 31
South America, 40, 49
South Australia, 15, 22
Spain
  Catalonia, 42
Spain/Portugal, 44
Submarine ridges
  Chatham Rise, 15
  Kermadec, 15
  Meteor Bank, 44
  Nazca, 11, 33, 34, 35, 58, 59, 69, 90
  Norfolk
    Wanganella Bank, 22
  Sala y Gómez, 11, 34, 35, 58, 59
Suruga Bay, 27, 61
Taiwan, 27, 56, 67
Tasmania, 13, 15, 22, 53, 60, 65
Tokai Aquarium, 26, 67
Turkey, 43, 52, 54, 55
Victoria, 22, 60
Western Australia, 23, 45
  Shark Bay, 22

MISCELLANEOUS

Allport, Martin, 15
Dimorphism, xvi, 8, 14, 30, 39
Early life history, 9, 20–21, 26, 43
Ecological notes, 21, 43
Ecology and ethology, 14, 26–27, 39
Eocene
  southern England
    Lower Eocene, 42
    Upper Eocene, 42
Ethology, 21
Günther, Albert, 15
Lectotype, designation, 19, 38
le Gras, M. G., 31
Length/weight relationships, xiv, 34, 90
Midlateral body scales, xiii, 5, 7, 48, 74, 77
Nasal lamellae, xiii, 73
Nasal organ, 2
Otoliths, 42, 58
Parin, Nikolai Vasil'evich, 34, 53
Plate, Ludwig Hermann, 40, 60
Pliocene
  late, 50, 53
  Zanclean Stage, 42
Pseudobranch, xiii, xiv, xv, 46–48, 76
Reproduction, 20, 43
Sexual dichromatism and dimorphism, 20, 26
Sexuality, 8–9
Sexuality and dimorphism, 42–43
Sexuality and reproduction, 30
Sexuality and sexual dimorphism, 34
Tectonic plates
  African, 49
  Antarctic, 49
  Caribbean, 49
  Cocos, 49
  Eurasian, 49
  Indo-Australian, 49
  Nazca, 49
  North American, 49
  Pacific, 49
  Philippine, 49
  South American, 49

www.ingramcontent.com/pod-product-compliance
Lightning Source LLC
Chambersburg PA
CBHW061753260326
41914CB00006B/1095

* 9 7 8 1 6 0 6 1 8 0 5 3 2 *